Martin Phillips

Page & Screen

The Media Response
in GCSE English

Pearson Education Limited
Edinburgh Gate
Harlow
Essex
CM20 2JE

England and Associated Companies throughout the World

ISBN 0582-42703-7

First published 2000

Printed in Italy by G Canale & C.S.p.A.

The Publisher's policy is to use paper manufactured from
sustainable forests.

Designed and typeset by Oxford Designers & Illustrators.

Contents

Contents *continued*

Introduction

This book is about two things:

1 The mass media (newspapers, advertising, television and film)

2 Your GCSE English examination

You are already an expert on the first of these items if you believe all the surveys of readers and viewers carried out in recent years. Students at secondary school are said to watch about 24 hours of TV a week and to buy many magazines during the course of a year. If that describes you, then you know a lot about what we call "the media".

You almost certainly don't spend as much time each week on the second item – your GCSE in English. The aim of this book is to draw together certain things you know about the media and get you to think a bit more deeply about them. This will mean that you will enjoy them even more because you know a lot about how media products such as television programmes, newspapers and advertisements are made. It will also help you do better in your GCSE English examination.

All GCSE English syllabuses test your understanding of "media texts". In the media part of the syllabus, the word "text" does not just cover printed material. A "media text" is anything we read or watch, whether that is a newspaper or magazine, a film or a television advertisement. This book sets out a system which will help you to know what to write about to get the best possible marks in this section of your GCSE English examination.

Different examination boards test your understanding of media texts in different ways. Each Part of this book begins by explaining these different approaches.

Some key concepts or "big ideas"

Before exploring the three types of media text covered by this book we need to understand a few basic principles. It is helpful to realise that all media share some common features.

1 The media exist to communicate information to large numbers of people

So in all cases there will be a group of people who work together to make the advert, the newspaper or the film. The "information" might be designed to educate, to inform or simply to entertain its audience.

Selling a fantasy

2 Each media text will have been very carefully constructed

The production of a newspaper or a television programme aimed at a large audience involves the use of different types of technology. A lot of people will have been involved in decisions about what should go in and what should be left out. Finally, they will use cameras, computers, transmitters or printing presses to put together and then distribute the finished product. It is an expensive business.

3 Because it is the result of a complex process involving a number of people with different points of view, every media text is subjective

This is a very important point to remember. We sometimes hear comments such as "television is a window on the world". This is not helpful. It seems to say that what we are presented with by the media is real, with no interference from anyone. In fact people make decisions about what should go in and what should be left out. This is bound to have an effect on the way the end product turns out.

Let's take an example to illustrate what we mean.

On 14 January 1999 the impeachment trial of the American president, Bill Clinton, for crimes and misdemeanors, started in Washington DC. Both BBC television and Channel 4 from Britain sent cameras to film outside the Senate building. Each crew recorded the line of about thirty Americans queuing to get in to watch the trial.

The Channel 4 crew took a long shot which showed the queue and all of the Senate building. Thirty people looked very small against a large building and its surroundings. "Only a handful of Americans showed any interest in the proceedings" said the newscaster, as the picture of the queue was shown.

The BBC crew took their camera right up into the queue. The camera operator held the camera at waist height while some of the people who were queuing crowded round, filling the screen with bodies. "Dozens queued to get into the historic impeachment trial of Bill Clinton" was the comment of the BBC reporter. The same queue on the same day – but the choice of shot and the comment linked with it gave a very different meaning.

This is an extreme example of how people tell stories in different ways. But what you need to remember is that everything you read, see or hear is the result of choices made by different people, whether in a newspaper office, in an advertising agency or on the set of a Hollywood movie.

4 Different people in the audience will "read" media products differently

Audiences for media products are large. They are likely to be made up of people of different ages, sex, race, political viewpoint, religious belief and so on. So while some people will watch the television programme *Men Behaving Badly* and find it hilarious, others will find it offensive and trivial.

As long as enough people read the media text in the way the producers hope they will, things are fine. But if the producers get it wrong and spend millions of dollars on a film no one goes to see, there will be serious repercussions. To avoid such problems, producers will constantly research what their audiences think, like, buy, read or watch.

From these points we can see that there is a process which is the same for all media products. Very simplified, that process might look like this:

A group of people construct their product (or media text) using the appropriate technology	→	They sell, give or transmit it to an audience	→	The audience may buy, take or watch it … and will respond to it in some way (by buying the advertised product; phoning the BBC to complain, or ignoring it entirely)

Looking at how media are made

The purpose of this book is to help you look in more detail at that process; to see what points at each stage need closer examination to help us understand how the meaning of the media text is being made. Parts One, Two and Three concentrate on the work of different people in the media industry who have choices to make and explores how those choices can change the way audiences respond to what they see on the page or screen.

Your entire GCSE English course is about language and the way it can be used for different purposes. The media part of your course also requires you to study language – but what is sometimes called "media language". This book explores the different "media languages" which those people who work on newspapers, or in advertising agencies, or for film and television companies use to construct their messages. To help pin down what sort of things you should be looking for, each chapter will give you some key ideas and labels to work with.

Part One will give you a set of terms to help you think and write about newspapers, and **Part Two** will do the same for display advertisements. Those two types of media text share some of the same "language" because they are *page-based* media texts. They work mainly by organising words and pictures in a certain way on a page. Pages come in all shapes and sizes, and they don't just get printed on paper. The internet is made up of web "pages", so although we get to read them through a computer screen they have more in common with this book than they do with video or film. What all pages have in common is that they sit still in front of us. You can flick back to the previous page or you can skip forward. You can glance up and look out of the window, and when you look back the same page will be there waiting to be read.

Part Three will give you another set of terms to use when you are thinking and writing about film or television – which we call the *moving image* media. The language used by the moving image media is made up of sounds and moving pictures that appear on a screen. Things don't stay still – they move forward. If you look out of the window while a video is playing you'll miss something. Although you can "freeze" the pictures with the pause button on your remote control, fast forward or rewind them, they weren't made to be viewed in that way. They were made to pass before your eyes in a set amount of time.

DUAL CLIMATE CONTROL,
CRUISE CONTROL,
SUPERLOCKING DOORS
AND A LITTLE BUTTON THAT MAKES IT GO UP AND DOWN.

If Range Rovers didn't have air suspension they wouldn't be the best 4x4s in the world.
But of course they do and they are.

A striking display advertisement, a good example of page-based advertising

At the end of each Part there is a summary to help you remember the key ideas. Finally, each Part ends with a glossary of terms to explain the meaning of key words used in that Part. Whenever a word in the book appears in **bold** type, its definition will be found in the glossary.

Writing about newspapers for your GCSE examination

The aim of this Part of the book is to help you think about the way newspapers put across their message to their readers. When you have finished it you will be able to:

- describe certain things about the way newspapers are put together
- explain the various choices on offer to the people who work to produce newspapers
- see how the choices they make affect the way we understand the meaning of what is written

This will give you a greater range of things to say about newspapers, whether you are answering an examination question or writing a coursework assignment.

The actual examination requirements for writing about the media will be different depending on which examining board's syllabus you are taking. You may be tested on your understanding of newspapers in the following sections of the different syllabuses:

- AQA/SEG: Foundation Tier (Paper 5 Section A) and Higher Tier (Paper 7 Section A)

- OCR/MEG: Foundation Tier (Paper 1) and Higher Tier (Paper 3)

AQA/SEG and OCR/MEG will give you materials to read before the examination and then set questions to be answered in the exam room.

- EdExcel: Foundation Tier (Paper 3) and Higher Tier (Paper 5)
- WJEC: Paper 2 Section A. There is a Foundation Tier (Paper 2) and a Higher Tier (Paper 2)

EdExcel and WJEC will include the media materials on the examination papers listed rather than "pre-release" them.

- AQA/NEAB: The Media Texts are part of your coursework. If you choose to work on newspapers then you can also decide which papers and which aspects you would like to write about. (There are some suggested assignments for the AQA/NEAB coursework piece at the end of this Part.)

AQA/NEAB also set examination questions on "non-fiction texts" in Paper 1 Higher and Paper 1 Foundation (Section A on each paper). The work you will be doing in this Part will also help you to prepare for that part of the AQA/NEAB syllabus.

Writing about advertisements for your GCSE examination

The aim of this Part of the book is to help you think about the way advertisements work on the people who look at them. When you have worked your way through it you will be able to:

- describe certain things about the way advertisements are put together
- explain the various choices on offer to the people who work to produce advertisements
- see how the choices they make affect the way advertisements work

This will give you a greater range of things to say about advertisements, whether you are answering an examination question or writing a coursework assignment.

The actual examination requirements for writing about the media will be different depending which examining board's syllabus you are taking. Advertisements are likely to appear in the following sections of the different syllabuses:

- AQA/SEG: Foundation Tier (Paper 5 Section A) and Higher Tier (Paper 7 Section A)
- OCR/MEG: Foundation Tier (Paper 1) and Higher Tier (Paper 3)

AQA/SEG and OCR/MEG will give you materials to read before the examination and then set questions to be answered in the exam room.

- EdExcel: Foundation Tier (Paper 3) and Higher Tier (Paper 5)
- WJEC: Paper 2 Section A. There is a Foundation Tier (Paper 2) and a Higher Tier (Paper 2)

EdExcel and WJEC will include the media materials on the examination papers listed rather "pre-release" them.

- AQA/NEAB: The Media Texts are part of your coursework. If you choose to work on advertisements then you can also decide which ones you would like to write about. (There are some suggested assignments for the AQA/NEAB coursework piece at the end of this Part.)

AQA/NEAB also set examination questions on "non-fiction texts" in Paper 1 Higher and Paper 1 Foundation (Section A on each paper). The work you will be doing here will also help you to prepare for that part of the AQA/NEAB syllabus.

Writing about film or television for your GCSE coursework assignment

This section of the book will help you to think about the way film and television put across their messages. Only the AQA/NEAB syllabus offers you the opportunity to write about film or television so it is a coursework essay for that syllabus that this Part prepares you for. When you have worked your way through it you will be able to:

- describe certain things about the way film and television programmes convey meaning

- explain the various choices on offer to the people who make programmes

- see how the choices they make affect the way we understand their programmes or films

The information and tasks have been designed to pin down various aspects of the process of making film and TV programmes and give them labels. This will help you notice things you might otherwise miss. It will also give you some ideas as to what you should say about them to get good marks for your GCSE assignment.

The newspaper industry

300 years of news on the page

In the year 2002 the British newspaper will celebrate its three-hundredth anniversary – if you believe claims made about the *Daily Courant*. Some say the *Daily Courant* was published first in 1702. Others claim that the *Stamford Mercury* printed its first edition in 1695. Whichever is accurate, newspapers have been around for a very long time, especially the *Stamford Mercury* which is still being printed under that title to this very day.

For some years now there have been fears among newspaper owners that television and, more recently, the internet, would spell the end of the newspaper as we have known it for three centuries. But in 1999 there are still 10 British national morning papers, between them selling over 13 million copies a day. Of the people in Britain who are over 18, just over half read at least one national newspaper every day. So the industry is not quite at death's door!

The national papers are usually divided into two categories. The **tabloid** papers are sometimes called "the popular press". There are five tabloid papers. Of these, the most popular are *The Sun* and *The Mirror*. Between them they have a **circulation** of over six million copies per day. These two, along with the *Daily Star*, are often called the "red tops" because of the red **mastheads** they use. Although they do include some news, they also contain a lot of gossip about personalities, shorter articles and a large number of pictures. The remaining two tabloids, *The Daily Mail* and *The Express*, are sometimes called the **middle market** dailies. They sell just over three million copies between them and, as the nickname suggests, are aimed at the middle of the newspaper market. They contain a balance of news, photographs and **feature** articles. The tabloids have smaller pages than the broadsheets. It is easy to read them without having to fold them.

The **broadsheet** papers are aimed at people who like a more serious newspaper. The five "qualities" as they are sometimes called are *The Daily Telegraph*, *The Times*, *The Guardian*, *The Independent* and *The Financial Times*. They have many more news stories in them, covering political and foreign items which tabloids often neglect because they think their readers will not be interested in that sort of article. Their circulation is very much lower than the tabloids. *The Daily Telegraph* and *The Times* have the highest circulation of the broadsheets but even they do not get near to the size of circulation enjoyed by *The Mirror* and *The Sun*. The broadsheets have a larger page size and are more difficult to handle when you are reading them.

Circulation in March 1999:

Title	Circulation
The Sun	3,813,381
The Daily Mail	2,362,184
The Mirror	2,303,510
The Express	1,085,550
The Daily Telegraph	1,045,336
The Times	746,403
Daily Star	605,112
The Guardian	402,494
The Financial Times	385,803
The Independent	224,306

Notice that the tabloids and broadsheets have very different styles.

But the national dailies are only a part of the newspaper story. At national level there are nine papers published on a Sunday. At local level, there are nearly a hundred papers, serving major cities and their surrounding suburbs, which are sold daily, and over 400 regional weeklies. Finally there are all those newspapers which come through the door free because their costs are completely covered by advertising. Called "freesheets", there are nearly a thousand of these papers containing a little local news and a great deal more advertising.

So there is a huge variety of papers being read in Britain, but we now need to turn our attention to the sorts of things you might write about when you are asked to read them in a rather unusual situation – not reading for pleasure but reading for the exam! To do this, we need to look at the choices which journalists make in the process of writing and printing newspapers.

Words

Newspaper style

The first person whose work we need to consider is the journalist. It's the journalists who go out to cover stories and write the **copy** which will eventually appear as the stories in newspapers. Like poets, journalists use as few words as possible, but for a different reason. Poets are concerned about the rhyme, rhythm and imagery of their words. Journalists want to communicate facts and ideas to busy people, packing the maximum information into the minimum space and time. "Keep It Short and Simple" (**KISS**) is the advice journalists will receive from their editors.

The opening paragraph of all newspaper articles, whether they are written for the quality broadsheets or the "red tops", will try to hook the reader by telling them all the important information about the story. Journalists use what they call the "5Ws" to pin down the basic information:

Who? What? Where? When? Why?

They then add an H to remind them that they might also answer the question:

How?

In the past the opening paragraph of a news story was supposed to answer all six of these questions. Unfortunately that led to long and clumsy sentences so modern journalists don't usually try to get all 5Ws and the H into their opening.

Mini Assignment 1

Look at the following example from the first sentence of a story from *The Sun*.

> Mike Tyson was given back his boxing licence last night after a plea by Muhammed Ali.

The Sun, 20 October 1998

In this example the following Ws have been answered:

Who?: Mike Tyson
What?: his boxing licence
When?: last night
Why?: a plea by Muhammed Ali

continued

Mike Tyson floored

Mini Assignment 1 *continued*

Look at each of the following opening sentences. In each case work out how many of the 5Ws have been included:

> The father of a 27-year-old woman who disappeared from Sidmouth last month is appealing for renewed efforts to trace her.

Express & Echo (Exeter), 11 February 1999

> Scientists have come up with a formula to stop dunked biscuits ending up as a soggy mess in the cup.

The Sun, 25 November 1998

> An executive with a recruitment company has won about £150,000 after claiming she was forced out of her job when she had a baby.

The Daily Mail, 25 November 1998

> Fluorescent yellow balls are to be used in all Nationwide League matches over the winter months in an effort to brighten up matches for players, referees and spectators.

The Independent, 20 October 1998

You will notice that the first three sentences, taken from tabloid papers, are slightly shorter than the one taken from *The Independent*. When they are writing for tabloid papers, journalists will try to keep their sentences to about 20 words. Even when they write for the broadsheets their sentences won't usually be longer than 35 words.

Another distinctive feature of journalistic writing is the use of short paragraphs. When you plan essays for the GCSE examination your teacher will probably have advised you to plan paragraphs which develop a particular topic or discuss one idea from a short story. These will probably go on for at least six or seven sentences. But, for tabloid journalists, the target is to produce a paragraph which does not go over four word-processed lines. Many paragraphs are just one sentence long. Although broadsheet journalists do use longer paragraphs, they still don't make them as long as the paragraphs in most GCSE essays. There are two main reasons for this use of short paragraphs:

- short paragraphs make for easier reading
- paragraphs in newspapers look longer anyway because they are laid out in narrow columns.

When you write an essay, whether for your GCSE coursework or in the examination, you will probably have been advised to keep back some particularly vivid description to hold the reader's interest in the middle of your piece. You may even save a really good point to include right at the very end – a "twist in the tail" of a murder mystery, perhaps. But newspaper journalists put the most important information in the first paragraph. Their story will then gradually taper off so that the last paragraph contains the least significant material. They do this for two reasons:

- newspaper readers often scan articles and don't always read through to the end
- the story might be too long to fit the space available on the page. If this is so, the **sub-editor** does not always have time to read the piece carefully and cut out a few sentences here and there. The last paragraph, or maybe more, will simply be **cut**. If a story is written in this way – where it can be cut from the bottom without losing anything important – it is said to have "met the cut-off test".

Research Task

Read four news stories, two from the tabloids, one from your local paper and one from a broadsheet. Make sure each story has more than five paragraphs. Cut off the last two paragraphs from each. Now check to see if each story passes the "cut-off test".

Word power: fact or opinion?

The words journalists choose often do more than just tell you factual information. Examination papers which test you on your understanding of "non-fiction texts" will often require you to distinguish between *fact* and *opinion*. Although we might think newspapers deal mainly in facts, it is not always quite as simple as that.

Where they cover a political story, for example, it may depend on the political party they support as to which facts they choose to include. If the number of people on hospital waiting lists falls, a paper supporting the government (which will claim credit for achieving this) could say:

LABOUR KEEPS ITS PROMISE ON WAITING LISTS

But a paper opposed to the government could use the number of people waiting for a hospital bed to give a different slant on the story:

THOUSANDS STILL WAITING FOR BEDS

Quite often a newspaper article will tell you a lot more than what has actually happened. It will tell you what the paper thinks about the events.

Labour contemplates the Millennium on a visit to The Dome

Mini Assignment 2

Read the following opening from the main story, known as the **page lead**, in the *The Mirror* on 25 November 1998 and then complete the mini assignment:

Prince Charles and his mistress Camilla Parker Bowles will party tomorrow at Princess Diana's ancestral home.

Diana's Spencer family are said to be shocked by the "insensitive" decision. A source said: "They are appalled at the thoughtlessness behind the invitation and horrified that Mrs Parker Bowles appears to have accepted."

Charles and Camilla will sip champagne and listen to a musical recital at Spencer House, the London mansion owned by Diana's brother and sisters and Princes William and Harry.

Then Camilla – the woman Diana blamed for the break-up of her marriage – will toast Charles at what will be the fourth party to mark his 50th birthday. The bash has been organised by the Duke and Duchess of Devonshire and millionaire financier Lord Jacob Rothschild, who has the mansion on a 120-year lease. None of the Spencers has been invited.

1 List everything in this article which is a fact.

2 Like many stories we read in newspapers, this one takes sides. There are "goodies" and "baddies". We can tell who *The Mirror* thinks are the goodies and the baddies by the use of some carefully chosen **emotive language**. This is where words are selected because they will spark an emotional response in the person reading the story.

For example, in the first line, Camilla Parker Bowles is described as Prince Charles's "mistress". *The Mirror* journalist chose that word rather than "friend", "companion" or "partner" because "mistress" has a direct link to sex. "Mistresses" are women who men have sex with outside their marriage. Readers of the tabloid press will be very familiar with the word as stories of men and women being unfaithful to their partners are a regular feature of tabloid news. So Mrs Parker Bowles is associated with scandal from the first sentence.

a) What words or phrases does *The Mirror* use to imply that what Prince Charles is doing is unacceptable, silly or empty-headed?

b) What words or phrases does it use to make us feel sympathetic to the family of Princess Diana and – because of the way the story is presented – sympathy towards the dead Princess herself?

This story has been given a particular **angle** by the *The Mirror*. It would have been possible for another newspaper to present the Prince Charles story from a different angle. They could have written it as a report of the Prince having a happy 50th birthday and trying to put behind him all the sadness since his ex–wife's death. But that, of course, may not have made such an interesting news story!

Mini Assignment 3

1 Read the following "bare bones" outline for a sports story:

Ferguson, number nine, protests as McCoist, number sixteen, loses out for Scotland

The footballer Duncan Ferguson, aged 26, has been transferred from Everton to Newcastle United for £8 million. The deal was agreed between the business-men who run the two clubs, Peter Johnson of Everton and Freddy Shepherd of Newcastle.

The manager of Everton, Walter Smith, was not told about the transfer deal until after it had been completed. He was annoyed about this.

Ferguson will join up with Alan Shearer as the attacking front men for Newcastle. Ferguson will be paid £40,000 a week which is more than Shearer gets. Shearer hasn't scored for the last nine games.

There are rumours that Shearer will not stay at Newcastle and that he'll be sold for £15 million to enable Newcastle manager, Ruud Gullit, to buy more players. But the Newcastle chief executive has said: "The board of Newcastle United have signed Duncan Ferguson to partner Alan Shearer. The object of the exercise is to have two top-class strikers playing up front for Newcastle. Nothing else."

There are other rumours that Shearer told Ruud Gullit he wanted Ferguson as his striking partner.

Shearer has said: "All I want is to be part of a successful Newcastle team. I love this club in a way only a Geordie could understand".

2 Write your own story for the back page of a tabloid paper. It must be exactly 300 words. It must follow all the guidelines which you have been given so far. The language should obey the KISS rule. Most of the 5Ws and the H should be included early on. Sentences should be about 20 words or shorter. Paragraphs should be short as well. And, of course, it must pass the "cut–off test".

continued

Mini Assignment 3 *continued*

Your article must have a definite angle on the events, with "goodies" and "baddies". You could have Walter Smith as the good guy who is trying to get on with his job while his players are sold around him by businessmen. You could have Duncan Ferguson as the money-grabber and Shearer as the devoted local player. Another angle would be the incoming hero Ferguson who is needed to boost the goal-scoring because Shearer is over-paid but under-performing. You must make clear what your opinions are by the emotive language that you use.

Grabbing the headlines

Writing the headline for a story is a very skilful job. If "Keeping it Short and Simple" is the guidance for all journalists, writing the headlines takes the art of KISSing to the highest level. The people who write the headlines are the **sub-editors**, although the headline for the main story on the front page will probably be the work of the **editor**.

Whether they are designed for broadsheets, tabloids or local papers, all headlines try to do five things:

- Show how important the story is by the size of the headline and where it appears on the page
- Draw readers to the story by telling them briefly what it's about
- Indicate the newspaper's angle on the story
- Fit in with the overall page design
- When it is the front page headline, grab people's attention when it is on the news stand

The tabloids

Headlines vary in the tone they adopt. The tabloids, especially the "red tops", tend to bend all the rules of conventional grammar and standard English in their attempt to create clever effects. They are controversial, and often written to shock. Here are some classic examples:

HOD'S WAD GETS THE NOD (*The Mirror*)

(*The Sun*) **SACK AS A PARROT**

UP YOURS DELORS (*The Sun*)

(*The Sun*) **GOTCHA!**

The ex-England football coach, Glenn Hoddle received a pay rise.

Hoddle again, this time fired from his job as England coach.

The French president of the European Union, Jacques Delors, had upset *The Sun*.

An Argentinian battleship had been sunk during the Falklands war in 1982 with the loss of more than a thousand sailors' lives.

STICK IT UP YOUR JUNTA   *(The Sun)*

(The Sun)   **CLOBBA SLOBBA**

This Falklands headline appeared after a British forces victory.

This appeared during the NATO attacks on Serbia and its president, Slobodan Milosevic.

Some people would say they may be clever but they are in bad taste. Others would say these are "good" examples of headline writing. Even *The Sun* felt it had gone too far with **GOTCHA!** Although **GOTCHA!** is one of the most famous headlines of recent years, it actually only appeared on the front page of the first **edition** of the paper. When the fact emerged that over a thousand Argentinian seamen had died, the editor decided to change it to **DID 1,200 ARGIES DROWN?** This is still controversial.

UP YOURS DELORS certainly leaves readers in no doubt about what the paper thinks of the president of the European Union, especially when it was linked to a two-finger salute as the main picture. It fits in with a long history of anti-European opinion in many of the tabloids. But it, too, could be seen as being in bad taste. Calling the French "frogs", as the story did, might be taken as a joke in some circumstances but when it is splashed all over the front page of a national newspaper many would say it is out of order.

But whatever the final judgement about good or bad taste, these headlines are eye-catching.

Broadsheets

Broadsheet headlines still try to be punchy and to the point, though in a more moderate way than the tabloids. When the former Chilean dictator, General Pinochet, was arrested in London in connection with the torture and murder of hundreds of his political opponents, both *The Guardian* and *The Daily Telegraph* covered it as their lead story. They both tried to indicate the seriousness of the political row in their headlines:

The crisis over Pinochet

was *The Guardian's* headline, while the *The Daily Telegraph* went with:

Storm over Pinochet grows

The use of dramatic words like "storm" and "crisis" are the broadsheets' way of whipping up their readers' excitement! Newspapers also have different priorities. On the same day as these papers led with the Pinochet affair, *The Sun* devoted nearly all of its whole front page to one story: CHRIS EVANS' SHOCKING CLAIM "HALF THE BBC ARE ON DRUGS". Presumably the editor of *The Sun* thought that *Sun* readers would be more attracted by this news.

Headline writers can also choose from a range of techniques to grab people's attention. Here are a few of them:

Abbreviating names	Princess Diana was always just **DI** in the tabloids. Glenn Hoddle was **HOD**.
Using slang	Another tabloid favourite is the use of words that aren't standard English.
	Examples: **SHE'S A STUNNER. IT'S A BUMMER**

Parody	Taking a well-known phrase or saying and slightly twisting it.
	Examples: **STICK IT UP YOUR JUNTA.**
	SACK AS A PARROT
Incorrect spelling	**GOTCHA!** is a good example of this technique.
Rhetorical questions	Posing questions which don't need an answer.
	Example: When Tony Blair hinted that Britain might join the European single currency, *The Sun's* front page headline asked **"IS THIS THE MOST DANGEROUS MAN IN BRITAIN?"**
Rhyming	Using words ending in the same sound.
	Example: **HOD'S WAD GETS THE NOD**
Alliteration	Using words which all start with the same first letter.
	Example: **HAPPY HARRY'S HOWLER**
Pun	A play on words, usually to give a double meaning.
	Example: **HI, JACK** (when the Home Secretary, Jack Straw, returned having been out of the country for three days, unavailable for comment on an important issue)

And *The Sun's* **CLOBBA SLOBBA** combines a number of these techniques.

Research Task

Look at as many headlines as you can during the course of one week and see if you can find an example to go with each of the techniques listed above.

Mini Assignment 4

1 Go back to your news story about the footballer Duncan Ferguson's transfer to Newcastle United and write some appropriate tabloid headlines for it.

2 Look back at the story on Prince Charles's 50th birthday party and write some tabloid headlines which might have accompanied it.

Pictures and layout

Photos on the page

A classic news photograph: the funeral of US President John F. Kennedy in 1963

So far we've looked at the choices made about the words which appear on newspaper pages. But another very important part of the job of those who work on newspapers is the selection of photographs to accompany stories. They are important because they make the design of the pages more interesting. They can also influence the reader's attitude to stories before a word has been read.

There are three main types of photograph which appear in newspapers:

- Photographs taken at the scene of the story by a photographer sent to cover it. An example would be the prime minister emerging from 10 Downing Street to announce a general election. Photographers will be part of a scrum and will have to do the best they can in the few minutes available to get their pictures

- Photographs which have been set up after the event where the photographer is in much greater control of the picture composition. An example would be a local school student who has been awarded a place on a round-the-world expedition. These pictures are very often posed

- Photographs which were not originally taken as a news photo but end up in the paper because they are the only available picture. An example would be the school photograph of a missing child at the centre of a police search.

Research Task

Look through any national or local paper. Put each photograph in the paper into one of the three categories above, with a very brief note saying why you think it fits this description. Where you can't be sure which category it comes from, make a note of which type you think it is most likely to be and say why.

No one individual controls the way photographs are chosen for newspapers. At least three people can be involved in making some sort of choice:

- The **photographer** will have decided what to photograph – and how to compose the picture if there is time to do this. Photographers will take lots of pictures to increase the choices open to people further down the chain

- The **picture editor** can choose where to send the photographer in the first place and, having got the photographs back, looks through and selects which ones will be best to support the story

- The sub-editor fits the photographs into the overall design of the page. To do this they may **crop** them to emphasise a particular aspect of the picture, or even just to fit into the space available

Whereas not all news stories have photographs to go with them, all photographs will have some words which help to pin them down – or to give a meaning to them which wasn't really there in the first place. As the famous newspaper editor, Harold Evans, said:

> *The camera cannot lie: but it can be an accessory to untruth … Words can turn images on their heads: the photograph of a couple locked in an embrace may be captioned Love or it may be captioned Rape. Time and again in war both sides have used one and the same photograph to attribute crimes to the enemy.*
>
> *Pictures on a Page* Harold Evans 1978

The choice of the words that go with the photograph is thus a very important part of the way readers put a meaning on to it. In newspapers there are two main types of printed text which support photographs – the headline and the caption. The caption is particularly important as it can relate directly to the photograph, providing an interpretation of it for the reader.

Mini Assignment 5

1   Working with a partner, each cut out three photographs from a local or national newspaper. These photos should be more than just a close-up of a face. Try to select ones in which there are some objects and background as well as people. Make a note of the caption but cut it off the picture. Stick each photo on to a plain A4 sheet of paper. Your partner will need to do the same.

2   Swap your three photos with your partner. Write some captions which seem to fit the picture on the sheets you have been given. Also, make a note of the particular things in the picture which led you to think the caption would fit.

3   Now look at the actual captions which accompanied the photos in the newspapers. Were any of your captions close to the original? What elements of the photos did the newspaper highlight in their caption?

Mini Assignment 6

Go back to the article you wrote and headlined on the Duncan Ferguson transfer in Mini Assignment 3. Look carefully at the following photographs and select one you would use to accompany your story. Write the caption you would use to pin down its meaning and also a brief explanation as to why you selected this particular photo and caption:

Mini Assignment 6 *continued*

Page layout

The final choice made before a paper is finally sent for printing is the way the page is designed. This is done by sub-editors who use computers to **page set**. They will work with a page grid divided into a number of columns. If they want to make something have a really dramatic impact, like the main photo for example, then it can spread across a number of columns. The same will be true for a headline. Support stories, on the other hand, may only take up one column width.

The copy of the front page of the *Oxford Mail* (see page 28) gives you the set of terms used by the people who design newspaper pages.

Getting the page design right is vital. Research into how people read newspapers has shown that photos are almost always looked at first by readers of the paper. Also, headlines which are near photos are read more than those which aren't. In fact, from the information the researchers give, it seems that most people don't "read" a newspaper, they tend to just scan through it.

So designing the page is a constant battle to get the reader's interest in the first place and then hold on to it for as long as possible. Newspapers are also keen to develop their own particular style so that their readers feel comfortable with a familiar product.

Design is as much about taste as it is about following rules. And the taste and rules which govern the choices made in one country are not the same the world over.

Mini Assignment 7

Look at the two newspaper front covers on pages 29 and 30. You are unlikely to be able to understand much of the language but you will probably have guessed that they are newspapers.

1 How would you know it was a newspaper?

2 How many of the layout features listed on page 28 can you find on each of these papers?

3 Take a British national daily tabloid and list the similarities in layout with these two papers and then the differences you notice. (You will need to think about the terms used on the layout diagram.)

Masthead

Title reversed out

Earpiece area

Dateline

Cross references

Support story

Splash head

Underscored

Page lead (the main story)

Byline

Graphic

4-colour picture

Box rule around text

OXFORD MAIL

Thursday, August 19, 1999   30p   www.thisisoxfordshire.co.uk

WIN A BIKE
TURN TO PAGE 7 FOR TODAY'S TOKEN

PAGES OF JOBS INSIDE

INSIDE TODAY
MORE LOCAL NEWS THAN ANY OTHER NEWSPAPER IN OXFORDSHIRE

News
Community centre backs down over call for a ban on kids at bingo nights
Page 2

News
Oxford Mail readers to the rescue for the family of eye op girl Harini
Page 5

Music
Where can you find Gary Barlow, 911 and Caprice all together this weekend? Find the answer on...
Page 28

Sport
Peter Fear's disastrous start with United suffers another blow
Back Page

BEST RESULTS IN THE COUNTRY!

A-level aces bag six of the best

By MADELEINE PENNELL

TWO star A-level pupils earned six A grades each in Oxford, as teenagers around the country learned of their results today.

Charles Roddie, 17, a pupil at Magdalen College School, gained his super six in maths; further maths; chemistry; English literature; computing and physics – which he taught himself, studying in his own time.

Charles, who won a place at Trinity College, Cambridge, to do maths, said: "I did quite a bit of work towards the end to improve my results after my mocks. But I was not stressed, I was quite laid-back. I enjoyed some of it because I discovered things for the first time."

Charles, a keen violinist, is about to go to Oxford's twin town, Bonn, with the county youth orchestra. He was among eight Magdalen boys out of 75 who gained four or more A grades.

The school achieved 67 per cent A and B grades and 98 per cent A to E.

Andrew Halls, master of the school, said: "Charles has had the independence and the ambition to pursue a rigorous combination of subjects, as well as finding time to be one of the best string players in a very musical school.

Meanwhile, at d'Overbroeck's College, Oxford, Vava Gligorov, 16, gained As in chemistry; physics; maths; further maths; general studies and computer science and got an A at AS Level applied maths.

He will go to St John's College, Oxford, to study physics and is currently in Vienna with his parents.

He took the first half of his general studies A-level last year and scored full marks. In his appraisal he said of the school: "As far as maths and the natural sciences go, d'Overbroeck's has the best academic department I know. All the teachers take a great personal interest in the pupils."

Headteacher Sami Cohen said: "All our pupils have done very well. Our pass rate is just over 93 per cent with about 50 per cent getting As and Bs which is neck-and-neck with last year. Vava came to us on a scholarship when he was 14 having previously been to school in Vienna and he has proved that he has earned it."
● Voice of The Mail: Page 8

TOP MARKS: Charles Roddie scored six A-grade A-levels   Picture: Antony Moore

Justice petition takes off

HUNDREDS of *Oxford Mail* readers have signed up to our campaign for justice on behalf of jailed lifer David Blagdon.

More than 1,500 people have added their names to our petition calling on Home Secretary Jack Straw to release him.

David Blagdon was jailed in 1978 for setting fire to curtains and a pew at South Hinksey church, causing £1,200 worth of damage. He had just lost both his foster parents and his home. He has now been

FREE
DAVID BLAGDON
FIGHTING FOR JUSTICE
MAIL

in prison longer than many murderers.

Copies of our petition forms continue to arrive in every post, and because of the amazing response we are extending the deadline to September 4.

If you believe justice should be done, please sign up. You can get a form at our offices at Osney Mead, Oxford, or telephone 01865 425404. Completed forms should be sent to David Blagdon Petition, Features Desk, *Oxford Mail*, Osney Mead, Oxford OX2 0EJ.

● Blutbad in Berlin 3 Tote ● Geiselnahme in Hamburger SPD-Zentrale ● Brand-Anschläge auf türkische Geschäfte ● Krawalle auf unseren Straßen hören nicht auf

Schluß jetzt!

Kanzler, Herr Schily – halten Sie Wort! Terroristen haben bei uns nichts zu suchen!

Donnerstag, 18. Februar 1999, 70 Pf

Bild
UNABHÄNGIG · ÜBERPARTEILICH

Dramatische Szene vor dem israelischen Konsulat: Sanitäter und Feuerwehrleute kämpften um das Leben eines angeschossenen Demonstranten.

> "Wer unser Gastrecht mißbraucht, für den gibt es nur eins: raus, und zwar schnell!"
> *Gerhard Schröder, heute Bundeskanzler, im Juli 1997*

* * *

In Deutschland leben rund 600 000 Kurden. Die überwältigende Mehrheit friedliche Mitbürger. Doch rund 11 000 gewalttätige Anhänger der kurdischen Terror-Organisation PKK verwandeln unsere Straßen in ein blutiges Schlachtfeld, tragen ihren Bürgerkrieg in unser Land. Gestern die entsetzliche Eskalation: Drei Tote und 16 Verletzte beim Versuch, das israelische Konsulat in Berlin zu stürmen. Neue Geiselnahmen und Straßenschlachten.

Wann greift unsere Polizei endlich durch? Meist sah sie untätig zu, ließ Terror-Kurden nach Geiselnahmen sogar gegen freies Geleit ziehen.

Bundeskanzler Schröder kündigte gestern erneut ein hartes Vorgehen gegen Gewalttäter an – wie auch Innenminister Schily, der die konsequente Anwendung der Gesetze versprach – bis hin zur Abschiebung von Gewalttätern.

Im Klartext: Raus mit den Terrorkurden! Herr Schröder, Herr Schily: Halten Sie Wort! Der PKK-Terror in Deutschland – Seiten 2 und 3.

NACHRICHTEN

Arbeiterführer verhaftet
Bukarest – Der rumänische Bergarbeiterführer Miron Cozma wurde verhaftet. Er war wegen staatsfeindlicher Aktivitäten zu 18 Jahren Gefängnis verurteilt worden.

TV-süchtige Deutsche
Hamburg – Die Deutschen sitzen immer länger vorm TV. 1998 waren es im Schnitt 3 Stunden, 8 Minuten am Tag. 5 Minuten mehr als im Vorjahr.

Brasilien: 114 Tote
Rio de Janeiro – Blutiger Karneval in Brasilien: 114 Menschen wurden dabei ermordet.

Immer mehr Handy-Unfälle
Tokio – Die Handy-Telefonitis unter Japans Autofahrern sorgt für immer mehr Unfälle. Steigerung gegenüber dem Vorjahr um 15,3 %.

Papst-Worte auf CD
Ostfildern – Fast jedes Wort des Papstes aus dem Jahr 1998 ist jetzt auf einer CD-Rom nachzulesen – der komplette Jahrgang des "Osservatore Romano" in Deutsch (98 Mark).

Mädchen verstümmelt – Haft
Paris – Wegen der Beschneidung von 48 Mädchen aus afrikanischen Einwandererfamilien wurde eine Frau (52) zu 8 Jahren Haft verurteilt.

Dax, Gold, Dollar runter
Frankfurt – Börse: schwach. Dax: 4810,09 (– 94,59). Euro-Stoxx 50: 5330,01 (– 72,20). Renten: schwächer. Der Dollar fiel von 1,7533 Mark auf 1,7416 (0,8905 Euro). Gold kletterte von 16 292 auf 15 959 (8160 Euro). Dow-Jones (Eröffnung): 9272,32 (– 24,98).

TV-Tip
● "Perfect Love Affair", nostalgische Neuauflage eines Hollywoodklassikers. Reporter (Warren Beatty) verliebt sich in Sängerin (Annette Bening).

Heute ist der 18.2.
...vor 56 Jahren rief der damalige Reichspropagandaminister Joseph Goebbels (1897–1945) zum "totalen Krieg" auf. Nach der verlorenen Schlacht von Stalingrad wollten die Nationalsozialisten die Kräfte aller Deutschen mobilisieren. Tatsächlich gelang es Goebbels, erneut ein weiteres Mal auf ihre Treue zum "Führer" einzuschwören. In seiner Rede im Berliner Sportpalast fragte er das fanatisierte Publikum: "Wollt Ihr den totalen Krieg?" Die Veranstaltung endete im Beifallssturm.

© A. Brockhaus GmbH, Leipzig, Mannheim

Noch 317 Tage bis 2000

Metall: Schlittern wir in den Streik?
Der zweite Tag im Metall-Schlichtungs-Poker von Böblingen – laut Teilnehmern war die Stimmung eiskalt. IG-Metall-Chef Klaus Zwickel (saß nicht am Schlichtungs-Tisch): "Es ist eisig, drinnen wie draußen." Ob die Zeichen heute noch auf Arbeitskampf stehen oder der Tarifstreit beigelegt werden konnte, war bei Redaktionsschluß völlig offen: Ein Einigungs-Ultimatum der IG Metall sollte um Mitternacht ablaufen.

Baulandpreise ziehen wieder an
Die Zinsen sind günstig – aber das Bauland wird teurer! Im dritten Quartal 1998 lag der Durchschnittspreis mit 98 Mark pro Quadratmeter 10 Prozent höher als im Vorjahreszeitraum, berichtet das Statistische Bundesamt. In den alten Bundesländern kostete der Quadratmeter inzwischen durchschnittlich 116 Mark, in den neuen Ländern und Berlin-Ost 59 Mark. Für baureif erschlossenes Land werden im Schnitt 159 Mark (West) beziehungsweise 81 Mark (Ost) pro Quadratmeter verlangt.

Wetter-Chaos legt Deutschland lahm
Schneesturme, Gewitter, eisglatte Straßen. Der Winter legt Deutschland lahm. Bis zu 70 km lange Staus auf der A2 bei Bielefeld. Ganz NRW schlitterte, Massenunfälle, viele Tote. Auf der A8 krachten 80 Autos ineinander. Flughäfen wurden gesperrt, Züge kamen nicht, ganze Strecken gesperrt. In Sachsen-Anhalt und Thüringen fielen Strom und Fernwärme aus. Ein Orkan zerstörte Häuser auf Norderney – Millionenschaden. Großer Bericht – Seite 7.

Öcalan
Das Video seiner Verhaftung

Von HAMDI GÖKBULUT

"Aufnahmen vom Terroristen-Führer." Unter diesem Titel verbreitete der türkische TV-Sender TRT gestern weltweit Bilder von PKK-Chef Öcalan auf seinem unfreiwilligen Flug von Kenia in die Türkei. Das Videoband wurde an Bord gedreht – der Beitrag, 6:36 Minuten lang, wurde stündlich wiederholt.

Öcalan ist mit Handschellen gefesselt, seine Augen sind verklebt. Die Bewacher machen das Victory-Zeichen, klatschen sich in Siegerpose ab. Öcalan spricht träge – wirkte wie ein gebrochener Mann. Stand er unter Drogen?

PKK-Chef Öcalan, in Handschellen gefesselt, er trägt eine Augenbinde. Er wirkt müde, benommen. 23.07 Uhr, die Bewacher sagen: "Du bist jetzt unser Gast. Herzlich willkommen in deiner Heimat."

Die Bewacher haben Öcalan die Augenbinde entfernt, sein Gesicht ist verzerrt. Die Bewacher fragen: "Wie geht es dir? Wenn es dir nicht gutgeht, holen wir nach der Landung einen Arzt, der dich untersucht."

Öcalan blinzelt in die Kamera, ein gebrochener Mann. Er sagt: "Ich liebe die Türkei, ich liebe das türkische Volk. Meine Mutter war auch Türkin. Wenn sie mir die Möglichkeit geben, will ich der Türkei helfen."

Die Bewacher haben ihre Gesichter mit Motorradhauben vermummt. Auf Öcalans "Hilfsangebot" sagt einer mit spöttischem Unterton: "Du kannst uns entgegenkommen, indem du unsere Fragen beantwortest."

Um 3.59 Uhr: Die vermummten Bewacher führen den geschwächten Öcalan quer durch das Flugzeug zum Bord-WC. Die Augenbinde wird ihm nicht abgenommen.

Die vermummten Bewacher in Sieger-Pose: Sie klatschen sich ab, einer spreizt später alle Finger zum Victory-Zeichen. Sie gehören vermutlich der Spezialeinheit an, die schon Öcalans Stellvertreter Semdin Sakik vor zwei Jahren im Nordirak festnahm.

COURSES
Dimanche à Vincennes
17 partants

P. I à VI

C'est la
saison des
CHAMPIGNONS
P. 18 et 19

SUPPLÉMENT
Aujourd'hui,
votre
TV Magazine

TV
MAGAZINE

Keri
Russel

FranceSoir

7 F 1,07 € Samedi 25 septembre 1999   Edition Nationale ● TIERCÉ

Mars : l'erreur de navigation

Pour 90 kilomètres,
après un voyage de
670 millions de km,
la sonde américaine
a fondu au contact
de la planète rouge.
Un fiasco de 750
millions de francs
pour la NASA   P. 2 et 3

Photo AP

L'enfant élevé par des singes

John, orphelin, a été recueilli par des chimpanzés   *P. 10*

Argent **P. 14**   Forme **P. 16**   Tourisme **P. 20**   Spectacles **P. 23 et 24**   Sortir **P. 25**   Télé **P. 26 à 31**   Jeux

News on the Net

It is said that we all live in "the information age". This means that we can now get more information about more things than any previous generation. The most important recent development is the internet (commonly known as the Net). This is really one huge electronic library filled with books, videos, CDs, magazines, newspapers – in fact *anything* which is reproduced to communicate with someone else is probably available on the internet somewhere.

The internet is a mixture of page and screen. But most of the information on the Net is actually presented in printed words and still pictures. You could make a copy on to paper of most **web pages** and they would be identical to any other paper page. The main difference between reading news on the Net and news in a newspaper is in how you get from one page to another. You can click on the "backwards" or "forwards" buttons on your screen to turn pages in the way you do in a book. But you can also press on certain words or **icons** on the page and it will take you straight to another page or even a completely different web site.

Journalists have had to adapt quickly to the internet because millions of people now regularly use it as a way of getting information about everything from the weather to the latest CD. Internet sites may have more errors as they are not always edited as carefully as newspapers. You should also check to see how recently they have been updated. Designers are faced with different problems and choices when making **web pages**.

First, the size and shape of the screen is different from a newspaper page. Although web pages can be scrolled using the computer keyboard, you can only see a limited amount of information at any one time. This particularly affects the use of photographs. Internet web pages have much smaller photos than are used to support the story in paper-based pages. It is also more difficult to read closely typed words from a screen than it is from a page, so more space is used around blocks of text and between lines.

Second, designers have to think about where readers might want to go from page to page. Newspaper readers can turn backwards and forwards quickly to find the information they want. So web page designers have to think about the layout of the page, and especially what they call the **navigation tools**. These are the buttons, icons and underlined words which enable readers to move from one part of the paper to another – or even to a different web site. For example, if an advertiser places an advertisement on a newspaper's web page, the paper can set it up as a **hot link**. With one click, the reader is transferred to the advertiser's own web site where there is more information about the product advertised.

One real advantage that web pages have over printed pages is that they are flexible. Newspaper web pages can include little audio or video clips which can be reached at the press of a button if you have the right sort of software. So not only can we read about what the Prime Minister thinks about the latest rise or fall in unemployment, we can watch a little clip of him actually talking about it in the House of Commons.

Research Task

Visit the web sites of some of the national newspapers whose web addresses are listed below:

   www.mirror.co.uk (*The Daily Mirror*)

   www.express.co.uk (*The Express*)

   www.guardian.co.uk (*The Guardian*)

Identify any of the layout features used on the web pages which have been borrowed from the way newspaper pages are designed.

Make notes on the main differences you notice between these web pages and a normal newspaper page.

What makes "good" news?

So far we have been looking at the choices made by individual journalists while they are writing their articles. But they will have already had to make a choice before they ever thought about which of the Ws to put in their opening paragraph. They will have had to decide whether to bother with the story at all – in other words, "Is it news?" The simple answer to this question is "It depends on what newspaper you're talking about". If your local council turns down a petition for a new swimming pool to be built in the town then that will probably be news for your local paper. But it's very unlikely that *The Sun* will include it.

There can never be an exact definition of what news is. But some people have tried to pin down the things that seem to make an event newsworthy. In a classic textbook for journalists written as long ago as the 1930s, an American called Curtis MacDougall listed the following five points for journalists to think about when judging the **news value** of any story.

News Values

1 *Prominence.* This is about the fact that some people are more well known than others. They are therefore more "newsworthy". What may be a common event in the life of an ordinary person becomes newsworthy if it happens to someone famous. So because David Beckham married Victoria (Posh Spice) Adams

continued on page 34

Good news for Posh and Becks?

continued from page 33

it was covered by every national paper and most of the locals, despite the fact that marriage is very common. If the leader of the local council gets married, she may be considered newsworthy enough for this to appear in the local paper but probably not in the nationals.

2 *Proximity.* This is about how close the story is to the audience that will be reading it. This is particularly important for local papers to judge. If your school receives a very good or a very bad report from OFSTED, the government inspection office, your local paper will probably cover the story. Every pupil at your school is likely to have someone at home who might read a news story if it was about their child's school. If a local group of people won £10,000 in the lottery it will be newsworthy for a local paper. But that story will have very limited news value in a town 50 miles away.

3 *Timeliness.* Journalists write about "news" not "olds". Newspapers concentrate on things which are happening at the time. So, although the disaster of a plane crash which kills many people stays with their families for ever, its news value will rarely go beyond a day or two. Crisis, drama and sensation are the stuff of news, and once the novelty has worn off so has the news value.

4 *Consequence.* Journalists and editors have to think about whether a story will have any longer lasting impact. The AIDS epidemic is an example of an event which, when it first occurred, wasn't well covered. It started in Central Africa. Western newspapers usually portray Africa as a continent with nothing but problems. But as AIDS wasn't the beginning of a drought which would lead to famine on a massive scale but merely an epidemic affecting relatively small numbers of people, it got little coverage. All that changed when AIDS spread to the western world on our own doorstep with devastating consequences.

5 *Human interest.* If a story has an emotional impact it may make it into the newspaper even if it doesn't have any of the other news values. If the editor thinks it will interest the paper's readers that may be enough. This explains how all those humorous or heart-warming stories about skateboarding ducks or children who have survived serious illnesses get into the papers. Giving stories a human interest keeps their readers' attention. "Fire sweeps through furniture factory" concentrates on the building but "Four hurt in factory fire" puts people into the story.

Research Task

Get a copy of a local and a national paper from the same day.

Does the lead story in the local paper get any coverage in the national paper? What do you think this story's news value was for the local paper?

Take a selection of stories from the two papers and see how many of MacDougall's news values criteria apply to each of them.

Newspapers: summary, assignments and glossary

Summary

This summary will help you to identify things you can write about when undertaking an examination question or coursework essay on newspapers. It is a very brief prompt chart of the main ideas you have studied in Part One, so if you are unsure what any of the points mean you should go back to the appropriate section and re-read it. You certainly shouldn't feel that you have to say something about each point on the list. Only write about those that are relevant to the analysis you are making.

Journalistic style	The extent to which any story answers the 5Ws and the H and whether all the important information is included in the first paragraph or two. The length of sentences and paragraphs
Headlines	How well the headlines work in grabbing the reader's attention. You need to consider the **angle** each headline implies to cover this effectively
Fact and opinion	The *facts* you find which are common to all three articles. Are there any things that ought to be facts that differ in any of the articles? The amount of *opinion* compared to fact each article contains. This is closely linked to the next point on the chart, *Angle and use of emotive language*
Angle and use of emotive language	The particular angle which is followed through in the articles. You should comment particularly on the material each paper has selected to support the angle it has taken, including any emotive language
Photographs	The photographs which each paper has used to support their story and the possible sources of these photos. How effectively the captions anchor down a meaning which fits the angle being taken in the story
Layout	The overall design of the page, including the balance of words to pictures, and how effective you think it will be in holding the reader's attention
News values	Why do you think this story was included in the newspaper? (Check MacDougall's list)

Assignments

Choose one of the following assignments for your GCSE English coursework folder if you are studying the AQA/NEAB syllabus.

Remember to use the appropriate points from the summary above to help you write it.

Assignment 1

Comparison of three tabloid front pages

Read the following three front pages from *The Express*, *The Mirror* and *The Sun*. Write a comparison of the way each has been constructed, and include similarities and differences.

Use the summary on page 35 to help structure your essay.

Thursday May 21 1998

The Mirror

www.mirror.co.uk   30p

FREE
MAGNUM Egg
ICE CREAM
Collect 2 tokens: See page 46

MY DARLING LUCY'S BACK

Grant's joy as his Saudi nurse bride comes home

WORLD EXCLUSIVE

By TANITH CAREY and NIC NORTH

THE husband of freed nurse Lucille McLauchlan told The Mirror last night: "My Lucy has been through hell — now she's coming home."

And Grant Ferrie said he plans to celebrate her return with a honeymoon — and a bacon roll.

Grant married Lucille, 32, six months ago as she languished in a Saudi Arabian jail, convicted with Deborah Parry over the murder of their colleague Yvonne Gilford.

The women flew out of Saudi's Dhahran airport late last night, looking tired and drawn and dressed in black islamic clothes.

They are due to land at London's Gatwick Airport early this morning.

Both were dramatically pardoned by Saudi King Fahd on Tuesday — 17 months to the day since their arrest.

Grant, 31, said: "Since we married we have had no more than two minutes alone — now

TURN TO PAGE 2

IN LOVE: Nurse Lucille McLauchlan and boyfriend Grant Ferrie pictured together before she went to work in the Saudi hospital where she met Deborah Parry — and Yvonne Gilford

THE Sun

Thursday, May 21, 1998   28p   **DEDICATED TO THE PEOPLE OF BRITAIN**

ZILLA CHILLA

We test new movie epic for shocks

CENTRE PAGES

WELL I'M BUNKERED

By BEN BACON

A SPORTS reporter joined England's soccer squad for a game of golf yesterday — and won a £189,000 Lamborghini Diablo.

New dad Derek Lawrenson, 38, received his black luxury sports car for a hole-in-one.

He was mobbed by his golfing partners for the day Paul Ince and Steve McManaman. Derek said after his ace at the 175-yard par three 15th hole: "Now I know how it feels to score the winning goal in the Cup Final. I felt like Gazza."

Sunday Telegraph writer Derek and wife Paula — who also have a BMW 318 — have a five-week-old baby, named Conor. Derek joked: "Unfortunately the baby seat won't fit in the Lamborghini."

Golf club makers Taylor Made sponsored the event at the Mill Ride club in Ascot, Berks — expecting the car to go to an England player, if anyone.

NURSES BACK TO MAKE A KILLING

Fury as murder pair cash in on story

Cell to sell . . . McLauchlan could earn £100,000

By SIMON HUGHES and MARTIN BENTHAM

TWO British nurses freed by Saudi Arabia after being jailed for murder were flying home early today into uproar over £100,000 payments for their stories.

Deborah Parry, 40, and Lucille McLauchlan, 32, were accused of cashing in on a colleague's killing by negotiating huge deals to tell all.

McLauchlan's representatives have already agreed a sum "upwards of six figures" to give her version of events to a newspaper. Parry's relatives were clinching a separate deal.

The payments were blasted by the family of Yvonne Gilford, the Aussie nurse the pair were convicted of murdering. Brother Frank said: "I suppose they will make a 20 million dollar film

Continued on Page Five

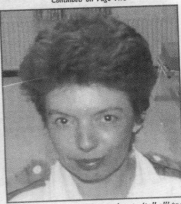

Blood money . . . pal Parry aims to 'tell all' too

THE ✠ EXPRESS

THURSDAY MAY 21, 1998   35p

HELP SAVE SUDAN: SCHOOL WALLCHART
• CENTRE PAGES

CHELSEA'S £10m SPREE
EXCLUSIVE • BACK PAGE

OUR GIRL IS NO KILLER

BATTLE: Deborah Parry

Freed nurse to clear her name

EXCLUSIVE
BY JOHN COLES AND MAGGIE MORGAN

THEIR dream has come true, their nightmare is finally at an end. After 517 days in a Saudi jail, Deborah Parry and Lucille McLauchlan will today set foot on British soil.

The two nurses, swathed from head to foot in black Islamic robes, were driven to Dhahran airport last night to board their flight to Gatwick, where they were due to

IN HER OWN WORDS
DEBORAH PARRY'S STORY STARTS TOMORROW ONLY IN THE EXPRESS

land at 6am. But for Deborah — clearly exhausted by her ordeal — and her family, the battle to clear her name has just begun. "This has destroyed my reputation," she said. "But I have a clear conscience and will hold my head high."

Deborah and Lucille were jailed 17 months ago after the murder of fellow nurse Yvonne Gilford. Deborah, 39, the more fragile of the two, suffered immense physical and mental stress as she faced the prospect of public beheading. She told her family from prison:
TURN TO PAGE 4, COLUMN 4

YES, WE'RE UNITED: Mo Mowlam and Richard Branson hit it off in Belfast yesterday

Branson in poll plea to Ulster

BY SARAH WOMACK
POLITICAL CORRESPONDENT

TONY Blair last night made his final push in the Ulster referendum campaign with a hand-written pledge to wavering voters.

With the clock ticking to tomorrow's poll, he made an 11th-hour plea for a Yes vote against the backdrop of a poster in his own handwriting.

Virgin boss Richard Branson rammed home the message when he joined Ulster Secretary Mo Mowlam on a walkabout in Belfast.

He pleaded for a Yes vote which he predicted would bring a surge of prosperity.

Mr Blair set out five pledges to the people of Northern
TURN TO PAGE 2, COLUMN 2

WEATHER 2 • OPINION 30 • LETTERS 32 • HICKEY 35 • TV GUIDE 56-58 • YOUR STARS 59 • CROSSWORDS 62 • CITY 64-66

Assignment 2

Comparison of any two or three newspaper front pages from the same day

This assignment is similar to Assignment 1, but it allows you to choose your own newspapers. You could vary it by choosing a day when the papers have different lead stories, allowing you to comment on and compare the different news values of the contrasting stories.

Assignment 3

Comparison of local and national newspaper front pages

For this assignment take papers which covered different stories on their front pages. Make one of the papers a local paper. The points to consider could include:

- the **news values** you think apply to each paper's stories
- the balance of serious to lighter weight news
- how effective you think the newspaper is in terms of the overall page design. There is no right or wrong answer to this – it is what you prefer. You must, however, make sure you give a detailed account that shows you know the layout choices which were available and why you prefer one design over the other(s).

Assignment 4

Comparing internet newspapers with their printed equivalents

For this assignment take just one newspaper and compare the way it is presented in its printed form with the way it appears on the internet. If you do this you will mainly be writing about the *design* of the paper. You will need to consider:

- the changes it has been necessary to make to convert the printed page into an internet page
- which stories have made it through to the home page of the internet version
- what information has been included in the internet version which was not in the printed paper and why

You could start with any of these three on-line newspapers:

www.mirror.co.uk (*The Mirror*)

www.express.co.uk (*The Express*)

www.guardian.co.uk (*The Guardian*)

If you prefer, you could choose another paper to make your comparisons by using a search engine to find its web address.

Assignment 5

Comparing the different approach to layout in different countries

If you are feeling adventurous, you could try working up Mini Assignment 7 (page 27). This will mean you are comparing British papers with some from other countries. This would be "adventurous" because you will probably only be able to comment on the layout. (If you are good at a particular foreign language then this might be an interesting assignment because you could start to comment on the language as well as the layout. You could discuss difficult vocabulary with your modern languages teacher – thus also improving your foreign language as part of your English GCSE.)

For the assignment to go beyond simple description you would need to speculate on what these different layouts might imply about what readers in the different countries have come to expect from their newspapers. You should say what differences you detect as well as things which newspaper readers appear to have in common regardless of their nationality.

Glossary

angle	the particular view a newspaper takes on a story which shows its opinion about the people or events reported on
broadsheet	newspaper which is printed on large sheets of newsprint measuring 117 cm x 82 cm. Sometimes called "quality" papers, they are bigger in size and weightier in content than the more popular tabloids
circulation	the number of copies that a newspaper sells
copy	the written words which appear in newspapers
crop	cut off parts of a photograph to emphasise one point or to make it fit the space available
cut	removing words, sentences or paragraphs from a news story
cut-off test	the test is to cut off paragraphs from the bottom of articles and see if they still get across all the most important information
edition	newspapers can change the contents of one day's issue, making a different edition of the paper
editor	the person in overall charge of the newspaper's content
emotive language	where a word or words are selected to spark an emotional response in the person reading the story
feature	an article in a newspaper which goes into greater depth than a news report

hot link	any button or underlined word on an internet web page which allows the reader to go instantly to a related web site
icon	an image which represents a feature, e.g. up, down
KISS	stands for "Keep It Short and Simple". Guideline given to journalists to make them write briefly and clearly
masthead	the title of the newspaper printed on its front page
middle market papers	the two tabloids, *The Daily Mail* and *The Express*, which are aimed at the middle of the newspaper market, targeting those people who prefer less gossip and more news but not of the serious kind offered by the quality broadsheets
navigation tools	the various buttons and icons on an internet web page which enable readers to get to different parts of the web site
news value	whether a story has enough interest to include in a paper will depend on its news value
page lead	the main story on the front page of a newspaper
page set	the process of designing newspaper pages using computer software packages which let you manipulate text and pictures
picture editor	the person responsible for selecting which photographs will be included in the newspaper
red tops	the most popular three tabloids, *The Mirror*, *The Sun* and *Daily Star*. They are known as the "red tops" because they use a red masthead
sub-editor (or **sub**)	person responsible for checking journalists' stories, deciding where they will appear in the paper and designing the pages on which they appear
tabloid	newspaper which is printed on sheets of newsprint measuring 58 cm x 41 cm. This is half the size of the broadsheet.
web pages	the pages which appear on screen when you are looking at the internet

The advertising industry

Display advertisements

'Wall to wall' advertising

Advertising is *very* big business. Its purpose is to encourage us to buy things or to think about things in particular ways. The advertising industry spends billions of pounds every year and employs thousands of people. Their job is to try to mould our behaviour. Researchers reckon that we have over 1,500 messages aimed at us every day. On the radio, through your letter-box, on the pages of your magazines and newspapers, on billboards in the streets, on buses and trains, in the supermarket, on the television … there's no escape. You are completely surrounded. The fact that there is so much advertising around means that the advertising industry has to come up with ever more sophisticated ways of grabbing our attention.

In this Part of the book we are going to be looking at one particular type of advertisement called the **display** advertisement. These are the advertisements you find in newspapers or magazines. They often take up half or whole pages. They are designed to attract the reader's attention immediately. In this respect they are different from the **classified** advertisements, or "small ads", which involve readers searching through columns of small print to buy things like a second-hand car or washing machine. Like most other forms of advertising, whether on the television, radio or on the printed page, the display advert will try to do two things:

- draw attention to the advertisement to make people look at it
- conjure up a certain emotional response towards whatever it is selling

When you write about adverts in your exam or for your coursework you will need to answer the *How* question: how does it grab your attention and how does it stir your emotions? To help you do that, this chapter will point out the various ways in which adverts are put together so that you have a checklist of possible things to look for when you are writing about them.

Who makes an advertisement?

Advertisements are designed and placed in the media by advertising agencies. Each advertising campaign will involve a number of different people. The following chart shows how an advertisement is created.

CREATING AN ADVERTISEMENT

● **The client**
It all starts with the client. This is the company or organisation that wants to advertise itself or a product it makes. The marketing department of the client organisation will go to an advertising agency and pay them to come up with the ideas for a campaign.

● **The account team**
The client deals directly with the **account team**. The account team find out all the about the product – who buys it, who might buy it and what it is the client hopes the advertisement will do.

When they have a firm idea about what the client wants, they draw up a brief setting this out clearly. They then set about market research. This will give them information about the people who buy similar products and also people who don't buy them. From this research, the account team write a marketing strategy which sets out the aims of the campaign. They take this to discuss it with the **creative team**.

● **The creative team**
The creative team turns the ideas into an advertisement. It's their work you will be studying when you write about advertisements for your GCSE examination.

The first stage for the creative team is to decide on a strategy. This will be a broad idea of what the campaign should be; how much should appear in printed media (newspapers, magazines, posters) and how much should be on radio or television. They discuss this strategy with the client and adapt it if the client is unhappy with the balance which they suggest.

Next they write and design an advertisement. The **copywriter** thinks up slogans. The **art director** draws on paper a design showing how the whole advert will look on the page. (If it is a television advert they will prepare a storyboard and a script at this stage.) From these initial ideas they produce a **scamp**, which is a rough sketch with just the main slogan on it, and an illustrator creates a **finished rough** with enough

detail to show to the client for approval.

An important part of the campaign is the **presentation** to the client. The creative team show the client the finished roughs and explain to them their thinking about how the campaign should work. They hope that the client agrees!

Once the client has approved the campaign, **photographers** and **graphic designers** produce the finished advertisement.

● **The media planning department**
While the finished advertisement is being produced, the media planners draw up the **advertising schedule**. This is the list of **spaces** they think they should buy in newspapers and the **time-slots** to be bought on radio or television. These suggestions go back to the account team and the client for approval. When everyone is happy with the schedule, the **media buyer** then books the space or the time with the newspapers, radio or TV company.

The design process

Designing display advertisements

Every single part of a display advertisement has been discussed and debated. Nothing will have been included unless the creative team considers that it adds to the impact of the advertisement. Everything in the advert is there because the people who designed it think it will have an emotional impact or create a particular impression which will help sell the product or the idea.

Once the creative team has been given the agreed brief, they sit down and brainstorm ideas about how to present it. Eventually they will come up with the **concept** which will guide all the work they then do on the campaign or individual advert.

Different leaflets are designed to target different audiences

So what are the various elements that the copywriter and the art director have to think about when they design a display advertisement? Their choices are about the following four things:

1 *The pictures*. Photographs, drawings or diagrams selected to convey a particular message about the product

2 *The copy*. The copy includes all the words used in the advert; the slogan or headline, any other captions and the **body copy**. The words used must appeal to the people being targeted by the advert

3 *The type style*. Every word in the advertisement, whether it is the large slogan or headline or the small print, will have its own design. These designs are called **fonts**

4 *The layout*. This is about the use of space and the way in which the words and images relate to each other

These are the four things you will need to think about and comment on when you are answering any exam question or writing a coursework essay about advertisements.

Pictures in advertisements

Just Published,

THE SCOTCH CHURCH QUESTION; the LAW and the FACTS; with an APPEAL to the NON-INTRU-SIONISTS and Sir ROBERT PEEL,

By PACIFICATOR.

LONDON: Hatchard & Son, 187, Piccadilly.

LONDON & BIRMINGHAM RAILWAY.

THE Public are informed that on and after Saturday, 1st April next, a TRAIN will LEAVE the ROADE STATION for London, at Half-past Seven o'clock every morning, Sundays excepted.

By Order,
R. CREED, Secretary.

Office, Euston Station, 18th March, 1843.

GEORGE COACH OFFICE,
NORTHAMPTON.

THE Public are respectfully informed that ON AND AFTER SATURDAY, the 1ST of APRIL, the ROADE COACH will LEAVE THE GEORGE HOTEL at 20 MINUTES BEFORE SEVEN IN THE MORNING (Sundays excepted).

Mr. HIGGINS, Proprietor.

The earliest form of illustration in advertisements

An Edwardian advertisement for cosmetics

Pictures are a very important part of most display advertisements. These can be drawings or diagrams but in most cases they will be photographs. It is the picture which attracts the readers' attention and encourages them to read more. This is especially important in magazines and newspapers because we tend to flick quite quickly through the pages, rather than read each page as we would if it were a novel.

The history of advertising has seen a major shift from printed words being the main feature to visual images being more important. The earliest surviving advert dates from 1477 and was a book promotion – Thomas Caxton's *The Pyes of Salisbury*. Early newspaper advertising looked very much like the adverts we still have today in the classified or small ads columns. There were no pictures and the whole advert fitted inside a one-column space. But as competition for products and services increased so did the need for advertisements to grab the attention and pictures began to make an appearance, as in the travel advertisements from 1843 shown on page 45.

By the end of the nineteenth century the picture was becoming a key part of advertising. In the advert on page 46 for female cosmetics we have all the ingredients of the display advertisement as it was to develop – a slogan, an image and body copy with the use of different **fonts**.

By the 1920s newspapers and magazines could use photographs and from then onwards the pictures became more and more important to the design of advertisements. By the 1980s advertisements for Benson and Hedges Gold and Silk Cut cigarettes took advertising to the point where they *only* used a picture, cheekily using the government health warning to tell people it was a cigarette advert.

It is the art director who will decide what the picture will be about and whether it will be a photograph or not. A quick flip through any magazine to look at the advertisements will tell you that they usually go for photographs. An art director explains the importance of selecting the right photographic image:

> What is the special quality that the right photograph can bring to a **graphic design**? Is it the ability:
>
> ✳ to describe,
> ✳ to convey atmosphere,
> ✳ to entertain,
> ✳ to make an artistic statement,
> ✳ or to sell a product?
>
> The commercial photograph can do all of these things. The reader already knows that the sparsely inhabited Caribbean holiday resort is likely to have silver beaches fringed with palm trees and a sea every shade of blue imaginable, all bathed in permanent sunshine. But did it ever look as enticing as in *this* photograph! The reader may already know what a souffle looks like and, indeed, may have cooked many. But doesn't *this* photograph make it look so delicious! … Most important though – it's a photograph so it *must* be real, even though the reality may be an idealised fantasy.
>
> It is this reaffirming of a dream, whether attainable or not, which makes the role of a commercial photograph so important. But the job of the photograph is not just to depict a familiar scene such as a holiday resort – it must also surprise and inspire, leading the reader with confidence into an unfamiliar idea, like trying out a different recipe or splashing out on the latest fashion or newest car.
>
> *Art Directing Photography* Hugh Marshall 1989

This photograph is designed to sell holidays

Of course photographs do not always deal in dreams. Sometimes they can try to conjure up nightmares. Look at the advertisement for Save the Children opposite.

The visual message is direct. Your emotional reaction is likely to have been immediate. So this image is working in a similar way to the picture of the Caribbean beach or the souffle – it is getting straight to a mood or feeling – but in this case it is a different mood or feeling that the designer wants you to feel. In each case it would have taken many more printed words to describe the scene or the person and that slower build-up may have meant the impact was less dramatic.

But the fact that photographs work quickly doesn't mean they are simple. To try to make sure that they have the desired effect on the people who will see them, the art director and the photographer will have planned everything down to the last detail. They know what each separate element of the final version will be contributing to the overall effect. Before we go on to look at the various choices they have to make, we need to think about exactly how photographs communicate their meaning.

In trying to unpick how photographs work it is useful to look at them on two levels:

- On the first level, we can talk about what is actually there in the photograph. This is about fact. It is straight description that everyone can agree on. This level is called the **denotations** in the photograph.

- On the second level we can move on to consider what the things we can see suggest to us. This might be different from one person to the next. We are moving into the realm of opinion. This level is called the **connotations** of the photograph.

KOSOVO CRISIS

Save the Children from violence

The war in Kosovo shows only to clearly how conflict and violence can threaten children today. Over half the population of Kosovo is under 18, so this conflict is hitting the young particularly hard.

Save the Children has considerable experience of working in troubled regions. That's why we have launched our 'Save the Children from Violence' campaign – to change government policy and raise money to help all children affected by conflict.

Active in the Kosovo area since 1993, we have increased our efforts to respond to the current humanitarian crisis. Working in co-operation with other aid organisations, we are distributing emergency parcels containing essential survival items – bringing desperately needed aid to young refugees in Macedonia, Albania and Montenegro.

We have also set up a registration service to help reunite children who have been separated from their families. And we are dedicated to giving children the long-term support they need to make a lasting recovery from the damage that has been done to them.

Your donation can help the children whose lives have been shattered by violence, homelessness and deprivation overcome the trauma they are suffering.

Please help us now

Save the Children, 17 Grove Lane, London SE5 8RD.
Registered Charity number 213893

£15 helps buy emergency kits, which contain: windproof jackets, warm socks, soap, towels, nappies and baby food.

£40 helps keep a truck delivering emergency parcels on the road.

Please return to:
Save the Children
FREEPOST
London SE5 8BR

Or call our 24-hour ansaphone
0171 701 0894

Or make a donation online
www.save the children.org.uk

£15 ☐ £40 ☐ £75 ☐ £100 ☐ Other £ ☐
*A gift of £100 or more qualifies for Gift Aid 2000, boosting it by almost a third
I enclose: Cheque/Postal Order/CAV/Giro No. 5173000 (payable to Save the Children)
OR charge my Mastercard/AmEx/Visa/Diners/CAF/Switch   Issue No. ☐☐

Account No. ☐☐☐☐☐☐☐☐☐☐☐☐☐☐☐☐

Signature_____ Card Expiry Date _____

Name (Mr/Mrs/Miss/Ms) _____

Address _____

_____ Postcode _____

PCS P574S SIC Telegraph 250x172

An effective advertisement to make us think

Mini Assignment I

Look at this photograph with a partner:

1 Write down the main things you can see in the photograph about which you think there can be no dispute. (These are the denotations of the picture.) Compare your list with the one made by your partner. Discuss any differences.

2 Now write down the mood or tone established by the photograph. You might like to jot down answers to the following questions. Where do you think the photograph was taken? Does the man look happy or sad? What do you think he is thinking? (These are the connotations the picture has for you.) Share your opinions with your partner.

3 Because advertisers want to try to narrow down the range of possible responses to any photograph they use, they will often use words to **anchor** it. Decide what sort of advertisement this image might appear in. Write a one-line caption to try to direct the way readers might respond to it.

In trying to make a photograph conjure up the desired reaction in the viewer, photographers will ask themselves certain questions: What should the model or models look like? What type of clothes will they wear? What will be the **location** for the **shoot**? What **props** will be needed? What camera and lenses will it be best to use?

It will be helpful if you think about the various choices which the photographer faces under two main categories. The first is the choice of people, objects and setting of the photograph. The second is the choice of techniques to be used when taking the photograph.

Discover the
freedom
(It's the perfect family holiday)

Imagine a holiday where up to four children can go free! With Keycamp your children can go free all summer and there's a free Children's Club on every campsite to help them make new friends.

✓ **Travel any day, any ferry**
✓ **115 sites in eight countries**
✓ **June holidays from £339**

Call today for a brochure or visit your local Travel Agent.

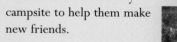 **0181 395 8565**
www.keycamp.co.uk

KEYCAMP
Holidays

Your key to the finest sites in Europe

People, objects and setting

The photographer and art director will choose the type of model or models. Then he or she will have to decide how to dress them, how they want them to stand or sit, what expression they want on the face, what other objects will appear in the photograph and where the photograph will be taken. Everything will be chosen to 'sell' the idea which the advertiser wants.

When setting up the photo shoot for the advertisement on this page, the following might have been the reason for some of the choices of people, objects and settings.

- The three children in the photograph are all looking directly at the camera. This is like most family snaps. Children and animals are often used for the "Aaaahh! Aren't they cute!" factor. Many adults will look at the children and find them appealing. This draws them into looking at the advert more closely.

- The casual clothes the children are wearing are associated with holidays. The fresh, bright colours fit in with the overall colour concept for the advertisement of blue and yellow – seen in the tents in the background of the main photograph, and the tent and caravan in the two smaller photographs of an actual Keycamp resort. The copy also uses blue lettering on a yellow background. The mum, dad and two children in the smaller tent photograph have been dressed to colour co-ordinate with the yellow/blue theme. The fact that the girl in the main photograph is wearing a sun hat, the young boy a sun cap and the older boy swimming trunks or shorts all supports the feeling of summer sunshine. This is reinforced by the very sunny conditions in the two smaller photographs.

- The facial expressions are very different; the taller blonde boy is almost laughing, the girl is smiling sweetly and the young blonde boy has a cheeky, mischievous look. The yellow cap on the young boy is set at a whacky angle to support the cheeky, expression. But they are all having a good time. They are grouped closely together to show that they like each other's company and – by association – they like being on the Keycamp resort.

- The children may have teamed up at the "free Children's Club". They are not with adults so the resort is safe enough to let children play on their own, giving both the children and – most importantly since it is adults who are the audience for this advert – parents the FREEDOM the slogan highlights.

• The two smaller photographs each show happy family groups enjoying themselves by playing and eating outside. Both tent and caravan are nicely spacious and well maintained and come with all sorts of outdoor furniture. The tent, in particular, seems to be set in its own field with no near neighbours to keep you awake at night arguing or playing loud radios. The sites themselves are very leafy, green, pleasant outdoor places.

All in all, the photographs have been carefully set up to give the message that Keycamp Holidays are just perfect for the family.

Mini Assignment 2

Analyse an advert of your choice by using the grid below to comment on the way it uses people, objects and setting:

Character type	The model will have been chosen to represent a particular type of person. How would you sum up the character type? How does this choice support the message of the advert?
Facial expression	How would you describe the expression on the model's face? Are the eyes looking directly at the viewer or at something else? What feelings do you think the photographer hoped to conjure up in the viewer through these facial expressions?
Gesture or posture	The model will have been given very careful instructions on exactly how to stand or sit, where to place their hands, the precise way to hold their head, etc. What do the postures and gestures make the viewer think about the model?
Clothing	Every article of clothing will have been carefully selected. Why do you think the model is dressed in this way?
Props	All the other objects, or props as they are called, will have been chosen because they support the overall message the photographer hopes to convey. What are the most important props? What effects do you think each prop was intended to produce in the viewer?
Setting	Whether the shoot took place on a specially constructed set in a studio or at an outside location, the setting will be used to add further to the overall effect of the advertisement's message. What effects does the setting in your advertisement summon up in the viewer?

The techniques to be used when actually taking the photograph

In addition to choosing the people, objects and setting, the photographer has another whole set of choices to make about photographic equipment and ways of using it.

First, they will need to think about the size of shot needed and the best type of lens to use. Shot sizes are usually described in four main categories:

Long Shot: always abbreviated to LS

The LS will include the whole of any person who is in the photograph and there will be a lot of information about the setting

Mid Shot: always abbreviated to MS

The MS will show the person from waist upwards. We will still be able to see some of the background but the person will fill much more of the photograph than they do in the LS

Close Up: always abbreviated to CU

The CU is where the head and part of the shoulders fills the photograph. It is a very intimate shot. It is as if we are standing very close to the person, staring them in the face. We can tell a great deal about the feelings of the person when a CU is used

Big Close Up: always abbreviated to BCU

In a BCU one part of the person completely fills the photograph. It shares the intimacy of the CU but can be used to narrow down the focus of attention and present things with dramatic impact

A wide- angle lens is used for this shot of car interior

The type of lens used is to some extent linked to the size of shot the photographer is aiming for. But different lenses will also produce different qualities in the finished photograph.

When a **wide-angle lens** is used, all the various elements of the photograph – the people, objects and setting – are in sharp focus (or **deep focus** as it is called). A wide-angle lens has been used to take the photograph in the advert above. In this advert, the lens makes the car look much wider and more spacious than it would be in reality.

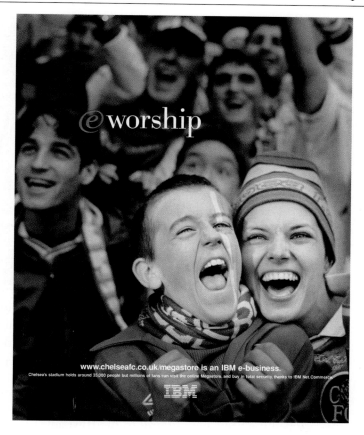

The effect in this photograph could have been achieved by using a **telephoto lens**. A telephoto lens enables the photographer to stand a long way away from whatever they are photographing while giving the impression of being a lot closer. They can also be used to create **selective focus**. This will draw the viewer's attention to one particular feature of the picture. In this case the two faces in the foreground are sharply focused in comparison with the rest of the image which is deliberately blurred. If a wide-angle lens had been used for this shot we would have seen the crowd more like a player would see them from the football pitch. By using a telephoto lens we feel we are right there in amongst the crowd.

Composing the shot

Once the photographer has decided on the shot type and the lens to be used, the next choice involves the way each object is placed within the frame of the photograph.

Sometimes a photograph will be a **symmetrical composition**. This is where the person or object being photographed is in the middle of the picture and the two sides are very similar to each other. Researchers claim that this sort of composition makes the viewer feel calm. It will often draw attention to the fact that it has been carefully posed for the camera. Symmetrical composition was often used by painters of religious scenes in previous centuries so there can also sometimes be a religious feel to whatever is being photographed.

The alternative is to use an **asymmetrical composition**. In this type of picture the subject of the photograph is placed to one side of the frame. This will tend to make the photograph look more natural, hiding the fact that, like all photographs taken for advertisements, it has been very carefully posed.

A good example of early symmetrical composition can be seen in The Coronation of the Virgin, *an altar piece by the Italian artist Giotto (1276–1337) in the Baroncelli Chapel, Sta. Croce, Florence*

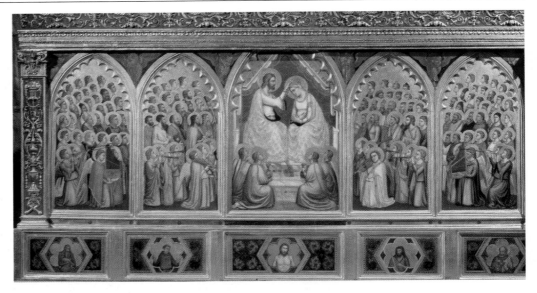

When they are thinking about how to compose a shot, photographers often talk about the **principle of thirds**. They apply the principle by imagining a grid laid over the scene they are about to photograph. The grid has two vertical lines and two horizontal lines which divide the picture up into equal thirds, like a noughts and crosses board. In an asymmetrical composition, the model would be placed on or near either the left-hand upright or the right-hand upright.

If we applied the principle of thirds to the IBM advertisement shown earlier it would look like this.

Principle of thirds

In the original photograph the two fans who are the main point of interest are placed on the intersection of the right-hand upright and the bottom horizontal line. The slogan has then been added near the intersection above and to the left. The points where the lines cross, called **hot spots**, are often used to place important elements of advertisements. So the two fans who are having a great time watching Chelsea are the hottest spot, followed by the hot slogan.

One final point to consider when thinking about composition: the "one photograph" may be made up of two or three photographs technically joined together to make it feel like one whole. From the point of view of getting the message across this doesn't matter at all. But it is interesting to try and work out whether the IBM advert was *really* taken in one go, "live" at a match – or whether the two "fans" were posed in a studio and their picture then superimposed on to a different crowd scene. And what about the sunlit forest outside the windows of the Volvo shown earlier? Has that been added afterwards?

Research Task

Take a selection of advertisements from newspapers and magazines and draw the "principle of thirds" grid on to them. Look at the hot spots and decide how anything placed there is supporting the main message of the advert.

Colour

The use of colour is an important part of the advertisement. A first choice for the photographer will be the type of **film stock** to be used on the shoot. The professional photographer has a huge range of film stock to choose from. One difference between the different types will be the film speed. "Fast" film doesn't need as much light to give a correctly exposed picture as "slow" film but it has a much grainier look to it than the finer, smoother look of slow film. But the most obvious difference – and the one which you will certainly want to comment on when you write your analysis of any advertisement – is the choice between black and white stock or colour.

Black and white pictures are considered to have a realistic feel to them. You might think this is strange because we see the real world around us in colour. This view that black and white photographs are somehow "realistic" probably comes from the fact that, until recently, all newspaper photographs were printed in black and white. Any family photographs you may have seen from your grandparents' days, and maybe even some early shots of your parents, are likely to have been in black and white. Also, documentary film footage from history, material from the Second World War for example, usually comes to us in black and white. So, although black and white is actually very unreal, advertisers use it to give a newsy, documentary, realistic feel to photographs. The makers of the IBM advertisement want us to feel that this is an actual shot taken at a match – something that might accompany a report of the game on the sports pages of a newspaper. This may be why they chose to use black and white film.

Where advertising photographs are shot in colour, they are quite often altered to emphasise one particular colour. To give a warm feel to an advert the red/brown/orange part of the colour spectrum will often be used. And if the advertising agency thinks a cool or cold feel suits the concept of the advert they will use the blue/green/grey colours.

Mini Assignment 3

Find a colour advertisement in which the colours have been tampered with in some way.

Write a paragraph describing the effect this use of colour has on the overall feel of the advert and explain why you think the art director decided to use colour in this way to sell the product.

Copy and type style

Copy

Slogans

The most important words in any display advertisement are the **slogan**. Slogans are similar to newspaper headlines. They need to grab your attention and hook you into the advertisement. Unlike newspaper headlines, however, some slogans are repeated endlessly so that we know them off by heart. And if we know them off by heart, the product will never be far from our mind when we are shopping! Some recent "classics" include:

It's good to talk *(BT)*

The fourth emergency service   *(Automobile Association)*

Just DO   *(Nike)*

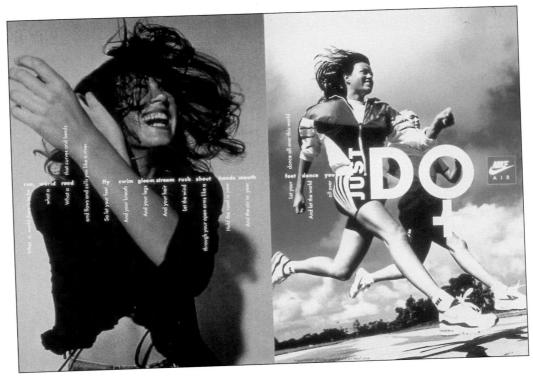

Like newspaper headlines, advertising slogans use a variety of language gimmicks. Some of the techniques will be similar to those we looked at in Chapter 2 when studying newspapers. Some of the following "tricks of the trade" are also used:

Clever use of language	This includes puns, jokes, reworking well-known phrases or sayings, or phrases with a double meaning
Using the sound of words	Using rhymes or words that all start with the same sound
Breaking rules	Using words or phrases with deliberate spelling mistakes or errors in grammar

Research Task

Find a range of advertising slogans. These don't necessarily have to come from display advertisements. You can write down any you hear or see on radio or television. Write a few sentences about each one saying how you think the copywriter is trying to make it memorable.

Body copy

As well as the slogan the creative team have to come up with the other words which will help to drive home the message. This will be the job of the **copywriter**. Sometimes they will only write a short phrase or sentence while for other adverts they might write three or four paragraphs. However many words are actually written, the body copy will have been very carefully worked on by the copywriter to ensure that it is doing its job. And its job is to make us a feel a certain way about the product.

Mini Assignment 4

Read this copy from a Sainsbury's advert:

> *The best time to pick a lettuce is early in the morning.*
>
> *Less heat and less sunlight means it can retain more moisture. More moisture means firmer leaves, fresher colour and a longer-lasting lettuce.*
>
> *Which is why all Sainsbury's lettuces are picked as early in the day as possible.*
>
> *And because our farmers take the same kind of care that you would, we like to think that our fruit and vegetables taste a little more home-grown.*
>
> *So if you want to be sure your lettuce is freshly-picked, pick one up at Sainsbury's.*
>
> *Sainsbury's. As good as home-grown.*

1 In no more than 15 words, write a summary of the main idea you think the copywriter was trying to get across in this advertisement.

2 Pick out the five or six key words you think are absolutely vital in getting this message across.

3 Compare your words with those chosen by a partner. Discuss any differences in word lists, explaining to each other why you thought particular words were essential.

4 Using a thesaurus, look up some alternatives for the key words and see whether you think the advert reads as well when you substitute the new words for the ones originally included by the copywriter.

5 The advert was originally a double page spread. The copy was on the right-hand page and the slogan and accompanying photograph were on the left-hand page. Write your own slogan and describe the photograph you would use for the advert.

One of the things a copywriter will have to think about is the way in which the advert will "speak" to its audience. They will often use the word "you" rather than "I" or "we" in their copy in an attempt to engage more directly with the reader. They need to work out what tone of voice they think will be most appropriate to create the right impression. Should they be chatty or formal, humorous or serious, knowledgeable, friendly? When considering the way to address their audience, copywriters use one or more of the following styles of writing:

Statement	"The cheapest baked beans you can buy."
Command	"Buy one today."
Question	"Can you afford to be without one?"
News	"Esso cuts petrol prices again."
Emotional appeal	"Your kids deserve to have the best money can buy."

Mini Assignment 5

1 Look again at the slogan and the copy for the Sainsbury's lettuces. Which of these five styles can you find in this piece of copywriting?

2 Find two or three advertisements with a slogan and only a few sentences of body copy. Identify the writing style the copywriter has used in each.

3 Using the five categories as models, try to rewrite the copy for each of these adverts in a different style than the original.

Type style

Each word that appears in the slogan or body copy of an advertisement has a design style. We call this style a **font**. The sizes of the letters in words are called the **point size**. There are thousands of different font styles and hundreds of point sizes.

This is Funstuff Bold	24 point
This is Bauer Bodoni	20 point
This is University Roman	16 point
This is Baskerville	12 point

The art director and copywriter will choose a font that they think suits the character of the advert they are designing. They may choose to put the slogan in capital letters or **upper case** as capital letters are called. However, research into the way people read in western cultures has shown that levels of comprehension are much higher when lower case lettering is used, so body copy will usually use a lower case version of the chosen font.

When writing your analysis of any advertisement you should try to describe how you think the character of the chosen font suits the overall design concept. This will be particularly important when discussing the slogan that is more likely to have an unusual design of font.

Mini Assignment 6

1 Which of the four font styles shown opposite do you think would be appropriate for the following types of advertisement? Try to describe the character of the font in your own words and say how you think it might fit the image of the product.

A new dance club

A firm of old, established solicitors

A new line of expensive chocolates

A new line of designer jeans

2 Compare your ideas with those of a partner.

Research Task

Collect a variety of unusual fonts from advertisements in magazines or newspapers. For each one write a one-line character description and list three or four other types of product which you think this font would suit.

Layout

The final job the art director has to do is fit the images and the copy together on to the page. This process is called **layout**.

There are no right and wrong answers as to where you should place pictures and where you should put headlines. In fact a lot of the features of design change as people strive for ever more interesting and arresting ways of setting out pages. In photography there has been a recent trend towards the use of techniques that would, in the past, have been considered to be just downright poor work. For example, off-balance compositions, blurs and over- or under-exposure are now trendy rather than shoddy.

But a lot of research has been done into the way that, in western cultures like our own, the human eye moves around a page. Because we read from left to right and top to bottom of pages, some researchers would have us believe that the most effective advertisement is one which takes us from the top left corner of the page to the bottom right. They call the point at which the eye first falls on the page the **primary optical area** or POA, so this would be the top left corner if the "rule" is correct. The last point the eye reaches is the bottom right-hand corner or the **terminal area**.

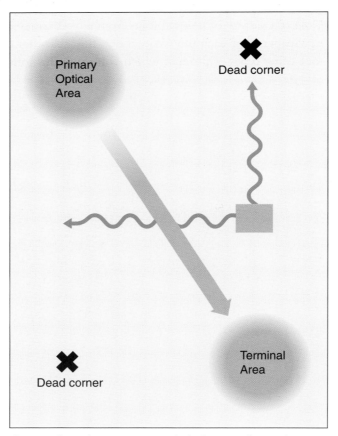

The wavy lines show movements which the eye will resist because they are going backwards

If this analysis of reading movement were to be strictly applied, then the "perfect" page layout might look something like this:

The ideal place to put the SLOGAN or HEADLINE would be here

Then you would have the copy in columns here. Then you would have the copy in columns here. Then you would have columns of copy here.

An image would go in this space

Then you would have the copy in columns here. Then you would have the copy in columns here. Then you would have columns of copy here.

Then you would have the copy in columns here. Then you would have the copy in columns here. Then you would have the copy in columns here. Then you would have columns copy here.

Then you would have the copy in columns here. Then you would have the copy in columns here. Then you would have the copy in columns here. Then you would have columns of copy here.

Then you would have the copy in columns here. Then you would have the copy in columns here. Then you would have columns copy here.

Then you would have the copy in columns here. Then you would have the copy in columns here.

Then you would have the copy in columns here. Then you would have columns of copy here.

Then you would have the copy in columns here. Then you would have the copy in columns here. Then you would have columns copy here.

Then you would have the copy in columns here. Then you would have the copy in columns here. Then you would have columns copy here.

Then you would have the copy in columns here. Then you would have the copy in columns here. Then you would have columns of copy here.

Then you would have the copy in columns here. Then you would have the copy in columns here.

An image would go in this space

Then you would have columns copy here.

Then you would have the copy in columns here. Then you would have the copy in columns here. Then you would have columns copy here.

Then you would have the copy in columns here. Then you would have the copy in columns here. Then you would have columns of copy here.

Then you would have the copy in columns here.

This theory obviously applies more to advertisements with a lot of copy. However it is also interesting to try and apply it to ads which rely mostly on a visual image.

Research Task

Collect a variety of display advertisements from newspapers and magazines. Try to find some which have a lot of written copy and others which are mostly image. See if you can work out whether they conform to the "rules" of page reading explained above. You might to try and mark on each advertisement the route you think your eye takes around the page.

The design for pages, whether they are display advertisements, magazine pages or books, will be mapped on to a **layout grid**. So the grid for the "perfect" page layout above would look like this:

The ideal place to put the SLOGAN or HEADLINE would be here	Then you would have the copy in columns here. Then you would have the copy in columns here. Then you would have columns of copy here.	Then you would have the copy in columns here. Then you would have the copy in columns here. Then you would have columns of copy here. Then you would have the copy in columns here.	An image would
Then you would have the copy in columns here. Then you would have the copy in columns here. Then you would have columns of copy here.	Then you would have the copy in columns here. Then you would have the copy in columns here. Then you would have columns copy here.	Then you would have the copy in columns here. Then you would have columns copy here. Then you would have the copy in columns here.	go in this space
An image	Then you would have the copy in columns here. Then you would have the copy in columns here. Then you would have columns of copy here.	Then you would have the copy in columns here. Then you would have columns copy here. Then you would have the copy in columns here.	Then you would have the copy in columns here. Then you would have the copy in columns here. Then you would have columns copy here.
would go in this space	Then you would have the copy in columns here. Then you would have the copy in columns here. Then you would have columns copy here.	Then you would have the copy in columns here. Then you would have columns of copy here.Then you would have the copy in columns here.	Then you would have the copy in columns here. Then you would have the copy in columns here. Then you would have columns of copy here.

Mini Assignment 7

Take two of the display advertisements you used for your research task which look very different. Draw on to them the grid pattern you think the art director used to set them out.

Advertising images

A question of audience

When Steven Spielberg was asked who he thought the core audience for his films were, he said "At this point, it's pretty much everybody...". Advertising agencies are not so lucky. They have to think very hard indeed about how the advert will be received by the target audience they are aiming to persuade, e.g. boys in their teens, girls in their teens, older well-off couples, etc.

A great deal of research has been done by the advertising industry into typical lifestyles of various groups in society. In the past a lot of advertising tried to target people by social class. There were six categories used to parcel people up into particular audience types:

A	High ranking managers in industry or the professions like law or medicine
B	Middle managers in companies or public services like health or education
C1	Junior managers or supervisors in industry or public services
C2	Skilled manual workers – like carpenters or electricians
D	Unskilled manual workers
E	The unemployed or others on very low incomes

Some products will be bought by all social classes. Washing powder, food, household items like chairs and cookers cross social class divisions. But as western countries became ever richer after the Second World War, there were many more luxury goods to be sold to consumers. Many of these items were way beyond the means of people earning C2, D or E level wages. So advertisers began to be particularly interested in getting their message across to the A, B and C1 categories.

Advertisers soon found that these broad social class categories were not sophisticated enough to distinguish between the various **niche markets** they needed to target to sell their products. The broad set of categories based on social class have been supplemented by all sorts of different classifications. These are often called lifestyle categories. The theory is that products are bought because of the lifestyle associated with them by the advertising campaign. So advertising researchers try to identify much more than what people earn; they try to find out about their needs, fears, hopes and goals in life.

One set of categories often used to define the younger audience outlook on life has the following descriptions:

Cowboys	People who want to make money quickly and easily
Cynics	People who always have something to complain about
Drifters	People who aren't at all sure what they want
Drop-outs	People who do not want to be committed in any way
Egoists	People who are mainly concerned to get the most pleasure for themselves out of life
Groupies	People who want to be accepted by those around them
Innovators	People who want to make their mark on the world
Puritans	People who want to feel they have done their duty
Rebels	People who want the world to fit in with their idea of how it should be
Traditionalists	People who want everything to remain the same as they are
Trendies	People who are desperate to have the admiration of their peer group
Utopians	People who want to make the world a better place

Advertisers don't expect us to fit one category and that's it. People can change and can also fit more than one category. For example, someone who is an environmental campaigner could be described as a "Rebel" and also a "Utopian". The categories are just helpful to advertisers when they are making distinctions between the various target audiences who might buy the product.

They can also be helpful to you when you are writing an analysis of advertisements because the way in which the photograph has been taken, the font chosen, the copy written and the layout designed will be largely determined by whom the advert is aimed at. One of the key things you need to do for Media work in English is to comment on the way texts (and a display advertisement is a text) work on their readers or audiences. By showing that you have thought about who might be the target audience for an advertisement you will be doing just that.

Research Task

Find two magazines on the same subject that you think would be read by different audiences. (For example, *Woman's Own* and *Red*). Make a list of the categories from the lifestyle list opposite which you think could apply to ten adverts from each magazine. Do you notice any pattern emerging in your two lists which might suggest that the magazines themselves might be aimed at particular lifestyle categories?

The world of the advertisement

At the start of this Part of the book we noted that we are surrounded by advertisements as part of our daily lives. Some people talk about the mass media as being a "consciousness industry". By this they mean that we are so soaked in images and ideas from newspapers, magazines, posters, television, radio and film that some of the ideas sink in and affect the whole way we think about the world around us.

The classic example of this drip-feed of images affecting the way we think about the world is the way that advertising images, and women's magazines in particular, present a totally unrealistic picture of the "ideal" woman's body. The models in all the advertisements are much thinner than the normal human figure. But this constant repetition of pictures of cleverly photographed skinny women dressed in the latest fashion means that being thin is associated with being beautiful. When this is backed up with film, pop and television stars who also look incredibly thin, the "consciousness industry" has affected our view of what a woman should look like.

We call this process of presenting similar images of individuals, groups of people or ideas **representation**. If the only images we see of black Africa are charity appeal photographs of starving people then we can develop a very narrow view of what being black and African means. This idea of representation links with what we have just been saying about "lifestyle" advertising. If we see representations of sports stars and other famous people using a particular brand of trainer then we can be persuaded that, to be trendy, we must also wear that type of trainer.

These are the simple examples. If we believe the idea that the mass media can affect our view of the world, there will be many parts of our way of thinking which might be subtly worked on by the barrage of images we are presented with in the worlds offered to us by advertisements. And these worlds, of course, are mainly designed to make us part with our money.

Mini Assignment 8

Find two of the colour supplement magazines that come with the weekend newspapers. One should be from a middle market tabloid like *The Sunday Express* or *The Daily Mail* and the other should be from a broadsheet like *The Observer* or *The Sunday Times*.

Mini Assignment 8 *continued*

Make a separate list for each magazine of all the products included in the display advertisements. Now group together any which are for the same type of product, e.g. advertisements for cars, holidays, perfumes, furniture. Put the products in a rank order for the number which appear in each magazine.

Flip quickly through each magazine to see if any of the articles are about things which are also featured as categories on your lists of adverts and make a note of these.

Write a paragraph or two describing the needs, interests and dreams the advertisers seem to think readers of each magazine will have.

Advertisements on the page: summary, assignments and glossary

This summary will help you to identify things you can write about when undertaking an examination question or coursework essay on display advertisements. It is a very brief prompt chart of the main ideas you have studied in Part Two, so if you are unsure what any of the points mean you should go back to the appropriate section and re-read it. You certainly shouldn't feel that you have to say something about each point on the list. Only write about those that are relevant to the analysis you are making.

PICTURES	
People, objects, setting	What is the audience going to think as a result of: the character types portrayed by the models; their facial expressions; their gestures or posture; the type of clothes they are wearing; any props in the picture; the location or setting which has been used?
Techniques	What is the effect of the type of shot (LS, MS, CU, BCU)? What effect has been achieved by the type of lens used? Why was the shot composed in this way? What effect does the colour design of the advertisement have?
Connotations	When all the above points have been combined, what ideas or emotions do you think the creative team hoped to conjure up by this picture?

COPY	
Slogan	How has the slogan been used to grab the reader's attention?
Mode of address	In what way and tone of voice does the advert "speak" to its audience?

TYPESTYLE	
	What effects do you think the different font styles were designed to have on the audience?

LAYOUT	
	How do the pictures and writing relate to each other? What route through the advert might a reader take? Why do you think the creative team designed the advertisement in that way?

AUDIENCE	
	Who do you think the target audience is for this advertisement? What supports this view?

REPRESENTATION	
	What "world" is conjured up in this advertisement? In trying to sell the product, what ideas and values are also being "sold" to us as desirable?

Assignments

Any of the following suggestions would make good media assignments for your GCSE English coursework folder if you are studying the AQA/NEAB syllabus.

Whichever assignment you choose, you should use the appropriate points from the summary above to help you write your assignment.

Assignment 1

Comparison of two types of display advertisement

Look carefully at the following two advertisements:

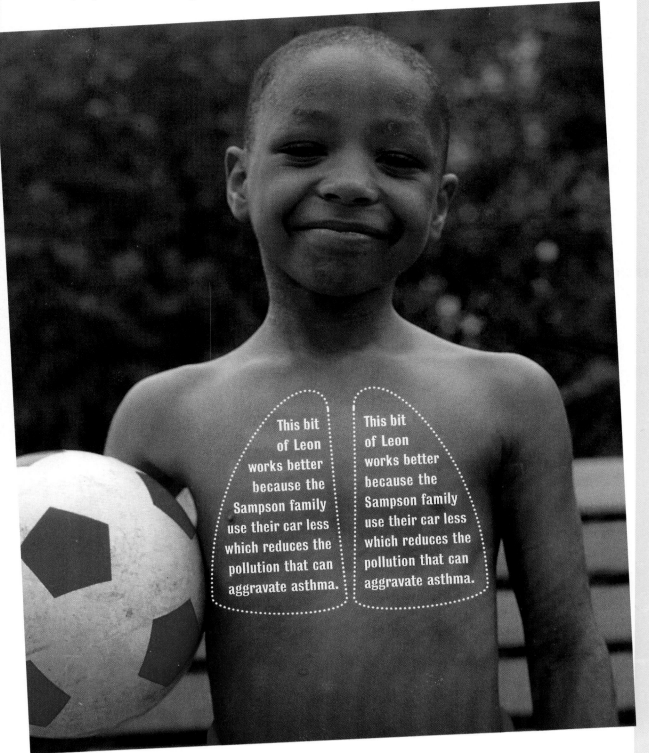

Assignment I *continued*

Wouldn't it be nice if everyone's body could be guaranteed for the next twelve years?

They are both partly to do with cars but one is trying to persuade people to buy a new car while the other is trying to persuade people to use their cars less.

What are the main concepts or "big ideas" around which the creative team has built each advertisement?

How do the various elements of photograph, slogan, copy and layout combine to try and get this idea across to readers in each advertisement?

Assignment 2

Comparison of two car advertisements

Look carefully at the VW Golf advert on page 75 and the Volvo S80 advert on page 54.

- What are the main concepts or "big ideas" around which the creative team has built each advertisement?
- How do the various elements of photograph, slogan, copy and layout combine to try and get this idea across to readers?
- What differences do you notice in the way the two photographs support the attempt to persuade people to buy the car?
- From what you have discovered from your analysis, what type of person do you think each advert is targeting as possible buyers of each car?

Assignment 3

Needs, interests and dreams

Develop further the work you did for Mini Assignment 8 (on page 70) on the lifestyle offered to us by certain advertisements. You should do this by giving a detailed analysis of individual advertisements and the patterns in the types of advertisements you found in the magazines. Build up a full picture of the needs, interests and dreams these advertisements aim to fulfil.

Glossary

anchor	a word is used to describe the way that a caption or slogan helps to pin down a particular meaning on a drawing or photograph
asymmetrical composition	the main subject of the photograph is placed to one side of the frame
body copy	the words which appear in an advertisement apart from the slogan
classified advertisement	an advertisement that doesn't use illustrations and requires the reader to search through columns of classified or "small ads" to find a job, buy a second-hand car or whatever
commercial photographer	photographer who makes a living by taking photographs, usually for advertising
concept	the overall idea behind an advertisement or campaign

connotation	the associations suggested to individual viewers by the content of a drawing or photograph
copy	all the words that appear in an advertisement
copywriter	the member of the creative team responsible for writing the words that go into an advertisement
deep focus	where everything in a photograph is in sharp focus, from the closest object in the foreground to the objects in the far distance
denotation	description of the content of a drawing or photograph in terms of what is actually there and about which there can be no dispute
display advertisement	an advertisement which takes up quite a lot of space on a newspaper or magazine page and involves illustrations and/or photographs as well as written copy
film stock	camera film is not all the same. You can use fast film for a grainier effect or very slow film for a sharper definition
font	the different styles of type used for the words in advertisements
graphic design	the process of selecting pictures and text (or copy as it is called) and designing the way they fit together into an overall page layout
hot spots	important parts of an advertising image are often placed on the intersections of imaginary grid lines which divide the picture into thirds, both vertically and horizontally
images	the images in an advertisement can either be photographs or they can be diagrams or drawings
layout	the process of deciding where the copy and the images will actually go on the finished page
layout grid	used to design pages, this is the set of horizontal and vertical lines set in a pattern on a blank page into which images, captions, copy and any other graphics are placed
location	the place where a photography shoot happens. There will be outside locations or studio work
lower case	description of letters which are not written in capitals (most of the letters in this glossary are lower case letters)
niche markets	particular groups of consumers within society who will be interested in buying specific products
point size	the size of letters in any font style, expressed as a number
primary optical area (POA)	the first area of a page that the eye goes to when looking at an advertisement

principle of thirds	a way of thinking about the composition of a photograph by dividing it into an imaginary grid, with three vertical columns and three horizontal rows, like a noughts and crosses board
props	any objects that need to be included in the photograph
representation	the way in which the mass media and advertising present, or *re*-present, images of certain individuals, groups or ideas to their audiences
selective focus	where only one part of a photograph is in sharp focus and the rest is blurred; selective focus is a way of drawing attention to something in the picture
shoot	the session where the photographer works in the studio or on location to photograph the images, one of which will eventually be used in the advertisement
slogan	the words that act as the headline for advertisements. Like newspaper headlines they are intended to grab the reader's attention
symmetrical composition	the main subject of the photograph is in the middle of the picture and the two sides are very similar
telephoto lens	a lens that enables the photographer to fill the entire frame with an object which is a long way away
terminal area	the last place the eye gets to before it leaves the advert
upper case	letters in capitals
wide-angle lens	a lens that takes in a great deal of the scene which is being photographed

"The Industry"

People involved in making film or television material do not want to draw attention to the fact that cameras, lights and microphones have been used to record the performance. We become so absorbed in the action we forget that someone has set it all up for the cameras. So those making the film or programme want us to concentrate on the story and not to think about the technical detail of how they have made it.

But the GCSE English assignment requires you to show that you have understood the way the various parts of a film or television programme have been stitched together. When working on other parts of the English syllabus you need to explain why you think Shakespeare chose certain words for a character to say, or why a poet selected a particular metaphor. You have to do the same thing with your media assignment. This Part of the book will help you to use "media language".

What is "the Industry"?

You will probably have heard people refer to the film or television "industry". They use the word "industry" because producing anything which is shown on a screen involves a large number of people and a variety of complicated technologies. The industry produces things to make money by entertaining, informing, or, in the case of advertisements, persuading us to buy particular products or think in particular ways.

A clock used to code the film at the start of a programme. It gives information on timing of synchronisation and the title

Think of the long list of **credits** which roll at the end of a film. Although the stars attract all the attention and earn a great deal of money, most people who work on movies are "behind the camera". Some have more influence on the final look of the product than others. **Directors** and **editors** are important. They have a big say in how a production develops. But there are dozens more who have worked hard in their own way to bring the film to the screen.

A television control room

Let's take an example. In 1996 Carlton Television made a TV version of a novel by Daphne du Maurier called *Rebecca*. At the end of the film the main characters return to their country mansion to find it in flames. The producers could have chosen to build a mock-up of the mansion and burn that down. Instead they decided to use flame troughs, smoke and lights to simulate a fire at a real country house and then to add some computer-generated images afterwards. The director discussed how to make it actually happen with the **director of photography** and the **special effects co-ordinator**. Once they had thought out where everything needed to be placed, they each called up their own teams to position the generators, lay hundreds of metres of cable, erect lighting stands and carefully set up the smoke and flame devices. There were over twenty technicians involved on the location to bring that one sequence from script to screen. And it took five hours to film it.

This house fire from Rebecca *is an excellent example of special effects*

Because it involves a lot of people and a variety of costly technology, making film or TV products is very expensive. The type of programme being made determines exactly how much it costs. Although television producers sometimes use what they call a "ball park" estimate of £1,000 for every minute which appears on screen, this can be misleading. Soap opera, for example, is much cheaper to produce than a TV advertisement. In fact the budget you'd need to make a 30-second advert would probably make five or six hours of *Coronation Street*. So you can see the attraction to TV companies of programmes like *You've Been Framed*. The content has been provided almost free by viewers!

Research Task

Look at the credits at the end of the next film you watch on television. If possible, record them on video as this will make them easier to deal with. How many people are credited with "behind the camera" jobs? See if you can work out what each of the people credited has actually done.

The early stages of production

Putting ideas on paper

In the early stages of any production a lot of things will appear on paper. For example, the **producer**, the person who is in overall control of all arrangements, will have written to a great number of people to set the process in motion. One of the first jobs is to find someone who will write the script or design the **storyboard**.

Screenplays

Screenplays are rather like play scripts except they include more detail about what will appear on the screen as well as the words spoken by characters. Screenwriting is the first stage of any production. Arthur Hopcraft earns his living as a screenwriter and here he describes exactly what his work involves:

"The screenplay is a fairly detailed description of what is going to appear on the screen. My overriding consideration has to be what is the film going to look like and sound like.

The screenplay doesn't look like a book. It looks like the text of a play. But unlike a stage play it has camera directions rather than stage directions. When you first glance at a screenplay it might appear as if there is very little being said because so much of it seems to be about where the camera is and where the people are moving."

Charles Dance and Emilia Fox in Carlton TV's Rebecca

Here is an extract from the screenplay which Arthur Hopcraft wrote for Carlton TV's *Rebecca*:

EXT. DAY. MANDERLEY. DRIVE

It is dark and menacing. It is so narrow that the car almost brushes the foliage on either side. Huge old trees make an archway that shuts out the light. MAXIM talks breezily – not noticing that DAPHNE feels the claustrophobic threat. She seems to shrink further into the bulky raincoat.

MAXIM

You won't have to worry about seeing to the house. Mrs Danvers is the one for that… does everything – just leave it to her… Quite a character in her own way… You'll probably find her a bit… stiff at first… But don't take any notice – it's just her manner…

DAPHNE is hardly listening – her eyes drawn to the dark, forbidding roof of twisted trees. MAXIM glances at her – cheerful smile.

MAXIM

Close your eyes – I'll tell you when to open them.

She shoots him a brave little smile, then shuts her eyes tightly.

CAMERA holds tightly on DAPHNE'S CLOSE-UP as the car slows to a stop – then suddenly MAXIM barks a command.

MAXIM

Now! Look !!

DAPHNE opens her eyes – they widen instantly in a sudden blaze of light. Her mouth opens in astonishment. CAMERA takes her point of view: the drive has widened to a towering avenue of brilliant, red rhododendron – huge crimson walls of them. Through the gap she sees the house.

MAXIM

Like it?

She can only gape.

Mini Assignment I

Take a key moment from a book which you are studying or have read yourself. The extract should be no more than a page long. Using the format of the screenplay above, turn the scene from your book into a screenplay.

(This piece could be entered for the Original Writing part of your coursework if it is good enough. If you are thinking of entering it then you would probably be best advised to use this mini assignment as a first draft and return to re-draft it after you have worked right through the whole of Part Three of this book.)

This is another example of fire as a special effect. This time it is being used in an advertisement

Storyboards

Not everything that appears on your television screen will have been written as a screenplay. Another way of planning what a piece will look like is to use a **storyboard**. This is a set of drawings which show exactly what each shot will look like and how the shots link together.

Storyboards can have certain advantages over screenplays. As they are drawings they can help directors to visualise what shots should look like in advance. They are also an easier way to communicate the ideas for the film to the whole production team. The great film director Alfred Hitchcock used very thorough storyboards to plan his films in minute detail before the shooting. He is quoted as saying that he felt that his movies were finished before they were ever made!

A storyboard from the James Bond film, Goldeneye

FINAL CONFRONTATION

191.

SINGLE
of
BOND
looking
up at
NATALYA

192

SINGLE
of
NATALYA
looking
back

193

INT.
ENGINE
ROOM
EXPLODES!!

Mini Assignment 2

Go back to your screenplay from Mini Assignment 1 and convert it into a storyboard.

From concept to camera

What we actually see on our screen will be the result of discussions between the director, who is in overall charge of camera work, acting and editing, and a variety of key people. We now need to look closely at who those other people are and, more importantly, what decisions they make which will affect the way the audience understands what is going on.

Shot types

A very important conversation will be the one the director has with one or more **camera operators**. They have a range of choices available to them in deciding what each **shot** will look like.

The first thing to decide is how close or how far away from the camera the person in the shot should appear to be. The choice made will depend on what the director wants the audience to know. There are three main types of shot which will form the majority of what we eventually see on screen:

Long Shot: always abbreviated to LS

The LS will show the whole of any person who is in the shot and there will be a lot of information about the **location** where the action is taking place. At the beginning of a new scene a director will usually use a LS as the first shot to establish the surroundings – which is why it is called an **establishing shot**. We feel detached from the action when we view the action in LS.

Mid Shot: always abbreviated to MS

The MS will show the person with their waist cut off by the bottom of the **frame**. We will still be able to see some of the background but the person will fill much more of the frame than they do in the LS. The classic MS is the TV newsreader in the studio, sitting behind a desk.

Close Up: always abbreviated to CU

The CU is where the head and part of the shoulders fill the screen. It is a very intimate shot. We feel very much a part of the action rather than detached from it. It is as if we are standing very close to the person, staring them in the face. We can tell a great deal about the feelings of the person when a CU is used. A slight raise of the eyebrow will be very noticeable, especially on a cinema screen where the face may be 5 m high.

In addition to those three types of shot, the director will sometimes choose shots that are a bit more extreme:

Extreme Long Shot: always abbreviated to ELS

Any person in an ELS will be very tiny indeed. The main thing we see will be the setting or location. The ELS will sometimes be used as an establishing shot.

Extreme Close Up: always abbreviated to ECU

In an ECU, one part of the person completely fills the screen. When an ECU is used it will have a dramatic effect on the person watching. It is as if you have thrust your face so close to the person on screen that your noses are touching. So, for example, an eye might fill the whole screen. Where you see an ECU, you should always ask yourself what effect the director was hoping to achieve by using it.

Camera angle

The next decision will be to decide the angle from which the shot will be taken. Here there are three choices from a TV series:

Eye level

This is where the camera is placed at about the height of the human eye. It is the angle used most of the time. This is because when we see an eye-level shot, we are less likely to be reminded that a camera has been present recording the scene. The signals going to our brain from the screen closely match the signals going to it when we look at anything else in the world around us in terms of the angle of view.

High angle

This is where the camera is placed higher up than the person it is filming. When we watch a high angle shot we appear to be looking down on the person in the shot. Towering over them in this way can often make us feel as if we are more powerful than the person on the screen. So if a dinosaur is attacking a person, the director might choose to use a high angle shot to look down on the person. We then seem to be the dinosaur dwarfing the frightened human.

Low angle

The opposite of the high angle shot, the low angle has the camera placed low down, looking up at the person in the shot. When we watch a low angle shot we feel dominated by the person on the screen who appears to be looming over us. So in our dinosaur example, if the director chose to use a low angle shot looking up at the huge dinosaur, we would feel like the scared person being attacked.

Lens movements

Sometimes the director will want the camera to be seen to move closer or further away during the filming of a shot. This will involve the use of the **zoom** device. If we get closer to the person, moving from MS to CU for example, the movement is called zooming in. Moving the opposite way, from MS to LS for example, is called zooming out.

Zooms will be another occasion when the director might want us to notice that a camera is present filming the scene, although the slower the zoom the less likely we are to notice it. When you do spot one, however, it is worth asking yourself why you think the director chose to include it. What effect does it have on you as you are watching it?

Camera movements

Finally the director can choose to have the whole camera move during the taking of a shot. The most common camera movement is the **pan**. This is where the camera moves from left to right or right to left.

Another camera movement is the **tilt**. This is where the camera moves upwards or downwards while filming.

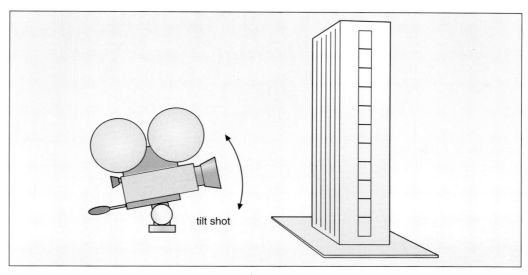

tilt shot

A camera dolly

Sometimes the camera will be placed on a **dolly** and moved alongside the action. An example might be someone walking or running along a road. This is called **tracking**.

In the 1970s the film director Stanley Kubrick developed another way of getting the camera to follow people around or move quickly through, for example, different rooms and corridors. The camera operator actually wears a heavy system of weights and brackets on which the camera is mounted. These keep it very steady and it looks as though it is on some sort of dolly as the movement is so smooth. Rather unimaginatively, the device was called the **steadicam** and is now in common use in both film and television.

The steadicam

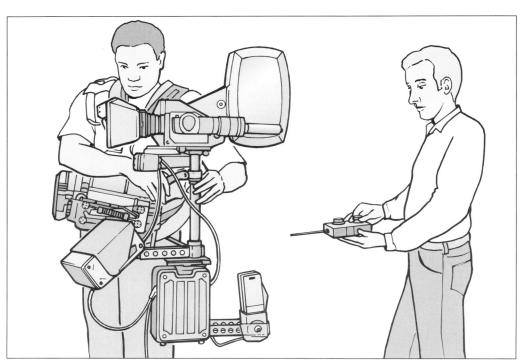

On some occasions the camera might simply be placed on the operator's shoulder and we see it following the person in the shot. This will give a very jerky effect and is often used to make it feel like the camera is the audience's eyes. This is called a **point of view (POV) shot**.

> ## Research Task
>
> Watch two different types of product on television – one should be a play, documentary, or film and the other should be an advert. Look for unusual shots, angles or camera or lens movements. Ask why you think the director chose to shoot it that way. In what other ways could it have been shot and why do you think the director decided it would not have been as effective?

Editing

From shots into sequences

So far we have concentrated on the individual **shots** which make up film or TV programmes. But these individual parts only make sense when they are joined together into **sequences**. It's a little like words building up into sentences. Each individual word may have some meaning. When we hear the word "man" we have some picture in our minds of a male figure. But if we add words either side of it, the meaning is much clearer. "The old man cried" gives us a much more detailed image to visualise. And of course if we put different words either side of "man", the meaning is completely different – "The young man laughed".

The joining together of the various shots into sequences is the job of the **editor**. Editing is a really important part of the whole programme-making process. The director will very often work alongside the editor because the choices made at the editing stage can completely change the meaning of the finished piece.

The following example should make clear how the order in which the editor chooses to place the shots can make a real difference to what we actually think is happening.

Imagine that each photograph is a shot. What do you think has happened in the first sequence? (opposite)

What do you think has happened in the second sequence? How has the meaning changed as a result of editing together the various shots in a different order?

This example shows a basic feature of editing. This is the fact that footage shot in completely different locations is joined together into one sequence. So in our example there may be three locations – first the place where we see the woman walking, second, the place we see the man walking and third, the place where they meet and shake hands. When shooting the material, the director would take all the shots of the woman on her own in one go. Equipment would than be moved and the shots of the man taken. Then the shot of the handshake would be the third location used. The sequence we see on screen would only be created at the editing stage. We get so used to seeing this technique that we don't see anything odd about it at all and we understand instantly what it means.

Sequence 1

Sequence 2

Let's take this a bit further. Look carefully at this series of drawings.

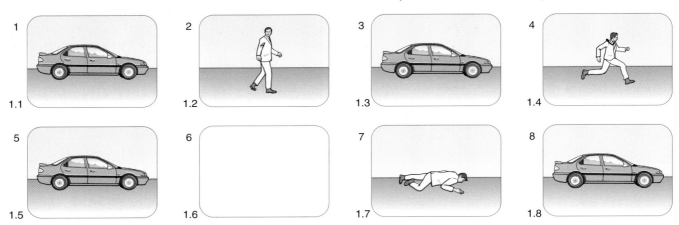

Imagine that each photograph is a shot. What do you think is happening in this sequence? What do you think we would see on the screen in shot 6?

Mini Assignment 3

You won't have had any difficulty in making sense of the edited sequence. But will everyone agree about what you thought was happening? To find out, compare your reading of it with that of a partner. Where were there differences? Explore the parts of the sequence that resulted in these different readings.

You may have noticed that the whole sequence was filmed in long shots. This didn't prevent you from reading a meaning into it. But it did leave you to use your own imagination to fill in the detail. For example, what expression is on the face of the running man? We can guess, of course, but usually a director would help us out by using different types of shot to give us more information. So in choosing which shots to set up, the sequence could have been filmed like this:

The reason that a director might choose this set of shots is not simply that it gives you more descriptive detail. As we have already seen in the shot types chart on pages 87–9, long shots tend to give you a much more detached view of the action. You are an observer. When we view close-ups, we feel much more a part of the action. This will make the action on screen seem more dramatic.

Mini Assignment 4

If you were directing the sequence of the car and the man, what other types of shot would you edit into the sequence to increase the drama still further? What would we see on screen in 2.8?

The final thing we need to think about is how long you would allow each shot to remain on screen. This will determine the **pace** of the piece. It would have a very different feel to it if each shot appeared on screen for one second, than if each was held for six seconds. The pace, how quickly or slowly the sequence seems to move, is always controlled at the editing stage as it is mainly about the length of time individual shots are kept on screen. **Rapid cutting** between shots would give a fast pace. It is used in chase sequences, for example, where directors and editors want to excite their audience. Rapid cutting is also very common in advertising, film trailers and pop videos. Where you want a calmer effect you are more likely to go for a slower pace.

Location or studio?

The sequences we have looked at so far would both be shot on location. With the man and car sequence, it would be possible to use more than one camera but often a location shoot would be set up so that the same camera filmed the series of shots.

Where a programme is made in a television studio, the set of choices is slightly different. Here the director may have three or more cameras all filming the same piece

This is the set of Neighbours

of action. This is certainly the case for chat shows and discussion programmes, and for most sequences in soap operas. In this sort of set up, the editing together of sequences is done at the time of filming.

The director will sit in the **gallery**, away from the studio floor, in front of a bank of television **monitors**. Each monitor will show the picture currently being taken by each camera on the studio floor. The director will then "call shots" to a **vision mixer**, saying which camera shot will be used. If this is the type of editing being used then the order of the shots – and probably the order of the entire programme – can only be changed if the whole thing is re-recorded. Although the process is different, the choices a director will make still follow the same principles of shot selection. As a general rule in soap opera, a sequence will start with an **establishing shot**. This will be a long shot showing us where the action is taking place. This is often followed by a series of mid shots or medium close ups where we see the character who speaks first, then a similar sized shot of the person they speak to replying, and so on. Programme makers refer to this approach as **shot/reverse shot**.

Research Task

Watch 10 minutes of any soap opera. Make a note of how many sequences follow the establisher/shot/reverse shot pattern. Try to work out how many cameras have been used to shoot the sequences and where these cameras were positioned.

Mini Assignment 5

For soap opera the director will try to cue the cuts between cameras from a pre-prepared script. Using the short piece of dialogue below, work out a camera script that would indicate exactly what shots will be taken by which camera:

Neighbours   Broadcast on BBC1 on 31.8.99

Scene involving three characters: *Lance (18-year-old boy)*
Julia (20-year-old girl)
Amy (18-year-old girl)

Lance: You've been on my mind a lot. That time, the time we had together. It meant a lot to me you know.

Julia: It meant a lot to me too.

Lance: And now here you are for just one day.

Julia: I wish it could be longer.

Lance: Guess we should make the most of it.

Julia: I agree. So why don't I freshen up a bit, and we can get going.

Lance: OK.

(Exit Julia to bathroom. Bell rings at front door)

Amy: Hi.

Lance: Hi.

Amy: You in the mood to celebrate?

Lance: Well, yeah.

Amy: Good, because I just got my first assessment as a fully fledged flight attendant! Oh, it rocked and I'm ready to party!

Lance: Oh, that's great and I'm really happy for you. (Looking at the bathroom door)

Amy: So you should be. So, what shall we do, I thought we could go and get the others and

(enter Julia)

…go to the pub. Oh, hi.

Julia: Now, you're not another sister, are you?

Amy: Sister?

Lance: No, no this is Amy.

Julia: Amy? Oh, Amy.

Lance: That's right, Amy.

Amy: Sorry, I didn't catch your name?

Julia: Sorry, Julia. Julia Burrows.

Amy: Julia, right nice to meet … Julia? Mildura Julia?

Julia: Yeah, that's me.

Amy: So, how did you guys meet? Lance never really told me.

Julia: Oh, my family owns the farm he was working on in Mildura. Sometimes I helped out with the picking and I ended up working alongside Lance and we just hit it off. Right from the start. I mean, he's such a charmer.

Lance: Ha, ha.

Amy: So, how long are you here for?

Lance: Not very long. So we'd better get a move on. We don't want to be late for that lecture.

Julia: Oh, no.

Lance: And, we've still got to check you into that motel, don't we.

Julia: I'll just grab my bag.

Amy: She seems nice.

Lance: Oh, she is.

Amy: So what do you reckon about getting together later on. You still interested.

(Lance looks confused)

To celebrate my good marks.

Lance: Oh, right, well there's Anne's exhibition and then Julia and I thought we might just see what happens.

Julia: We'll just play it by ear, hey?

Amy: Great. Sounds lovely.

Lance: So, you all set?

Julia: And raring to go.

(Exeunt)

Here is a plan of the set. Copy it. Now decide where you are going to place the three cameras available to shoot this piece. Draw them on to your floor plan and then carry on scripting, using the headings on the chart opposite. (The first couple of shots have been filled in as an example to help you.)

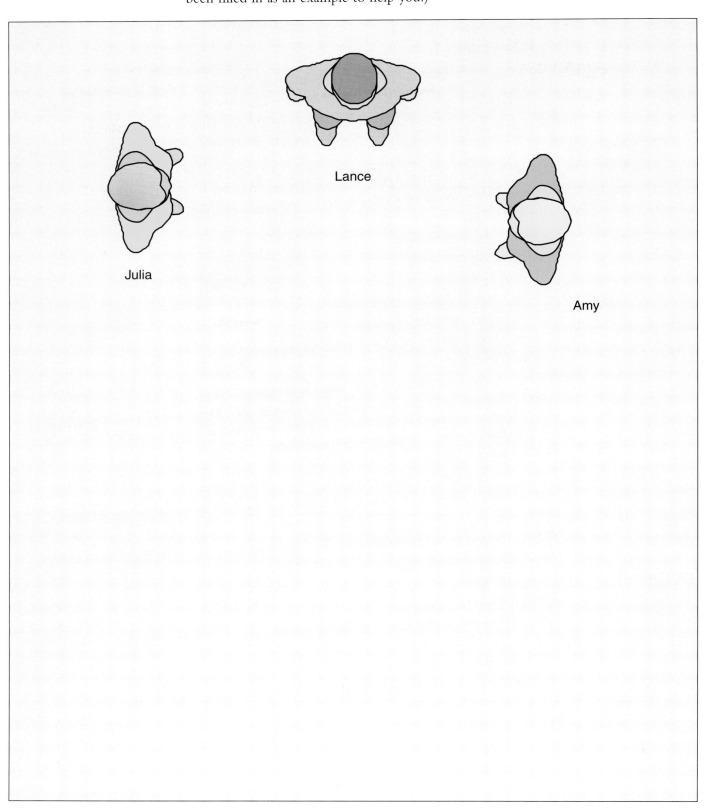

Lance

Julia

Amy

Soap Opera

Shot number	Camera number	Shot description (Use abbreviations)	Any camera movements	Dialogue spoken
1	1	LS (Lance, Amy, Julia)	Static	Julia: Oh, my family owns the farm he was working on in Miljura. Sometimes I helped out with the picking and I ended up working alongside Lance and we just hit it off. Right from the start.
2	2	CU of Julia	Static	Julia (cont): I mean, he's such a charmer. Lance: Ha, ha. Amy: So how long are you here for?
3	1	MS (Lance, Julia).	Static	Lance: Not very long. So we'd better get a move on. We don't want to be late for that lecture.

Abbreviations

CU	Close Up. A shot which shows a character's head and shoulders.
OSS	Over the shoulder shot. A shot that is made from over the shoulder of a character often with the shoulder evident in the frame. This is frequently used in conversation scenes.
2 Shot	Medium shot in which two people fill the frame.
3 Shot	Medium shot in which two people fill the frame.
Pan Shot	A shot where the camera moves horizontally and follows the subject.

Transition

The final thing we need to think about when analysing a sequence is the way we get from one shot to the next. In most cases the **transition** between shots will be a **cut**. But, as usual, there are a number of other choices about the transition a director can make.

There are five main types of transition as listed on the next page.

The cut

The cut is where one shot is instantly followed on the screen by another. This is by far and away the most common transition. It is so common, in fact, that when it happens we hardly notice because we are so used to it.

All the other transitions are much more likely to draw attention to themselves and so when you notice them it will be worth asking yourself the question "Why did the director choose to use that sort of transition rather than a cut?"

The jump cut

The effect of a jump cut is to make the character on the screen literally "jump" from one place to another. It also makes the person watching jump because it disrupts our illusion that what we are seeing is real life. A jump cut looks more like magic!

The dissolve

This is where the first shot gradually dissolves and is replaced by the second shot. There will be a moment when both shots are on the screen, before the first one gradually fades away.

The fade

This can either be a fade in, which is where a blank screen is gradually filled by the incoming shot, or a fade out where the shot gradually fades away, leaving a blank screen. The fade is usually used to show that, in the case of a fade in, a new scene is beginning, or with a fade out, that we have reached some sort of an ending.

The wipe

The effect of a wipe is to see the first shot chased off the screen by the next shot. Wipes can use all sorts of different patterns to get one shot off and the next on. The incoming shot can burst through in the shape of a star or the outgoing shot can appear to swirl round and disappear like water running down a plug hole. Wipes will definitely draw attention to the fact that we are going from one shot to the next.

Research Task

Watch one full advertising break during a soap opera, making sure you time how long the break runs. (It will be easier to perform this task if you can record the whole soap opera on video, including the commercial break.) Make a note of the total number of transitions made in the advertisements. Now take a section of the soap opera that lasts for the same length of time and count the transitions. Which had the higher number of transitions? Why do you think this might be?

Watch a further five minutes of the soap opera and see if any of the transitions are not simple cuts. Try to imagine a dissolve or a wipe replacing each cut in the sequences you have just viewed. What effect would this have on you as you watched it? Why do you think soap operas use the cut as virtually the only way of getting us from one shot to the next?

Lighting, colour and effects

In the light

Most things you see on film and television have had some sort of lighting added to them. You won't always notice that this has been done because the lights will often have been used to make the scene look realistic. But even shots taken outdoors frequently use extra lighting.

The person in charge of the lighting is called the **lighting cameraman** or director of photography. This person will liaise closely with the director, discussing the look of the shot and then working out the number of lights required and the best places to put them.

When thinking about the lighting of a shot they will start by considering three main positions.

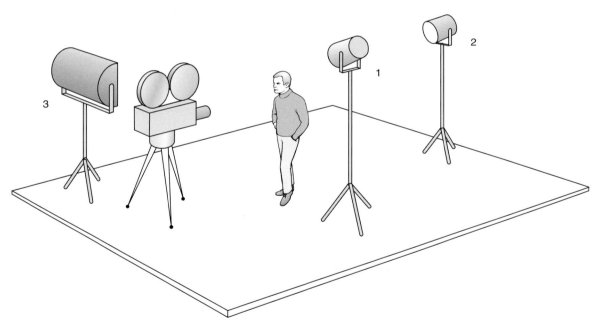

Three point lighting set-up

The choices they have to make revolve around which of these lighting sources to use and which to leave out. The combination they choose can make a great deal of difference to the look of the shot.

The photographs opposite give an idea of the effect these various lights might have on a scene.

Key light only

The **key light** will be the main source of light in the shot. It is usually set slightly to one side of the camera and directed at the person being lit. (When a shot is taken outside in sunlight, the sun can provide the key light.)

Key and fill light

The **fill light** is placed on the opposite side and is less powerful than the key light. It literally "fills in" the shadows created by the key light.

Key, fill and backlight

The **backlight** is placed behind the person being filmed. The purpose of this light is to separate the person from the background and give a three-dimensional look to the shot.

The final choice to be made about the lighting is how high or low to place the light. In general the light will be placed above head height shining down on to the person in the shot. This is because we are used to light from the sun coming from above and lights in rooms being on the ceiling.

From your point of view, when you are writing about film or television you probably won't find much to say when the lighting has been set up to give a realistic effect. Soap operas are usually lit realistically because the director wants the audience to think they are watching real life unfolding in front of their very eyes.

But when one or more of the lighting sources has been left out or positioned in an unusual way, then you will want to ask why the director has chosen to make you notice the lighting. When a shot or sequence has unusual lighting, or **expressive lighting** as it is sometimes called, this will often be because the director wants to set a certain mood or tone. Crime films will often have a dark and threatening feel to them created by the low levels of light the director has chosen to use when filming.

Looking at colour

Another choice to be made by the director is whether to shoot in colour or black and white. It is normal now to use colour most of the time both for television and film. But this certainly wasn't true for the first 50 years of cinema's history. The first television broadcast in Britain was in 1936 but it wasn't until 1967 that we had colour TV.

Strangely enough, films shot in black and white are often seen by audiences to be just as "realistic" as films shot in colour. This is especially true when the subject of the film is historical. Because we often experience historical events through old newsreel footage or black and white photographs, a black and white film seems more authentic. A recent example of a director choosing to use black and white film is Steven Spielberg in *Schindler's List*. As the film was based on the story of a real man, Oskar Schindler, who helped Jews to escape death in Nazi concentration camps during the Second World War, shooting it in black and white gave the movie a historically authentic feel. The film ends in the present day, however, so for the closing sequence Spielberg used colour film.

But there are more choices available than simply whether to use black and white rather than colour. It is possible to alter the way the colour looks on screen. For example, you can give a bleached effect to the colour by using a technique called **desaturation**. This can give a dreamlike quality to what we see on the screen. A director may give a warm feel to a scene by emphasising the red/brown qualities of the picture, while making more use of the blues will give a colder feel.

Research Task

Watch a variety of television advertisements and make a note of any which seem to have used colour in an interesting or unusual way. What effect do you think the director was trying to achieve through this use of colour?

Adding effects

There are two sorts of effects you can look out for in your search for things worth commenting on when you are analysing film or television. There are those to do with sound which are dealt with in Chapter 17. There are also those things that affect the picture.

Explosions are always dramatic special effects

Common visual effects include:
(a) desaturation; (b) saturation;
(c) distortion; (d) superimposition

Special effects are the responsibility of a trained, professional special effects co-ordinator. This person's job is to set up dramatic reconstructions of events such as car crashes or explosions. These need very careful planning and often involve stunt people who earn their living by doing dangerous things full time.

Visual effects are different. Rather than being filmed on a set or a location, visual effects are created in laboratories in the case of film, or through video effects equipment for television. Since the mid 1980s the development of electronic effects technology has had a big impact on the look of television, particularly youth television. Advertisements and pop videos are two areas where these visual effects have been put to a great deal of use. Some common visual effects you should look out for are:

desaturated colour (as described on page 107)

saturated colour (this is the opposite of desaturated where the colours are very vivid and unnatural)

slow motion

fast motion

distortions (the picture has been stretched or squashed)

superimposed images (where two or more images appear on top of each other).

Research Task

Watch at least 15 advertisements. Make a list of all the different types of visual effects you notice being used in them.

The soundtrack

Sound and meaning

Film and television don't just involve pictures – although that was true of film for the first 30 years of the history of the cinema, of course. But even in the days of silent movies people realised how important sound was to the meaning of the film. Their way of adding it was by having a pianist or orchestra playing along with the film as it was projected. Since those early days, however, in both film and video the soundtrack we hear is almost as important as the pictures we see. The two things work closely together to create meaning. In fact it's possible to give a completely different meaning to the same sequence of shots by adding a different commentary or piece of music to them.

To explore this idea, read through the following two charts. You will need to imagine the pictures that are appearing on the screen as described in the "visual" column. By comparing the different words and music in the "voice" and "sound" columns you will see how much the soundtrack is responsible for creating the meaning.

Shot no.	Visual	Voice	Sound
1	LS. Taken from out of the window of a train as it crosses a river. Jungle on either side	This is the Yahlu river, gateway to a secretive nation. It's a land which still bears the scars of American bombing in the 50s during the bloody war when West fought East for control of Korea	Sound of train wheels on the track beneath voice
2	LS. Also from the train window, we see a very large statue of an Asian man in a long military coat	Kim Il Sung is the ruthless dictator who has ruled over North Korea for a generation	Still train sounds
3	ELS. High angle shot of a very large city square with what look like ancient Chinese buildings around the edges. A large parade of people is marching across the square	The human ants toiling across Kim Il Sung Square are stuck in…	Sound of marching feet
4	LS. The parade of people march past the camera. They are in civilian clothes but they are marching in step	…an Orwellian nightmare where it is disastrous to be out of step	Fade up sombre marching music played by a military band
5	MS. Low angle. Children with smiling faces, dressed in traditional Chinese-looking costume, dancing in lines and waving at the camera	Kim Il Sung says these are the happiest people alive. In truth they are brainwashed and coerced into obedience	Music still heard faintly under voice. Fades out at end of shot
6	LS. Inside a shop selling radios and television sets. Lots of people browsing the shelves, looking at the goods for sale	It is forbidden to read or listen to news from abroad. Radio and TV sets are modified by the state to enforce that law	Sound of radio going on in the background
7	MS. Low angle. People on an escalator travelling downwards	Few North Koreans are allowed overseas and…	Sounds of escalator
8	LS. An underground railway platform with a train drawing in and people getting on and off	…travelling outside the capital city of P'yongyang is only allowed for Communist Party members or the military	Sounds of train station
9	LS. Low angle. Still in the underground, people pass in front of a huge and colourful painting on the wall. It looks like the same man as we saw in the statue	Even 300 ft beneath the city in the underground that doubles as air raid shelters, there is no escaping Big Brother	More sombre military music coming from speakers in the station

Shot no.	Visual	Voice	Sound
1	LS. Taken from out of the window of a train as it crosses a river. Jungle on either side	People looking for an unusual holiday in an exotic location…	Sound of the train wheels on the track
2	LS. Also from the train window, we see a very large statue of an Asian man in a long military coat	…will be well served by the distant land of North Korea, just opening up for tourism	Still train sounds
3	ELS. High angle shot of a very large city square with what look like ancient Chinese buildings around the edges. A large parade of people is marching across the square	The capital city, P'yongyang, is full of historic buildings dating back many centuries. Throughout the year you can be assured of all sorts of…	Fade up lively music played on oriental pipes and chime bars
4	LS. The parade of people march past the camera. They are in civilian clothes but they are marching in step	…colourful carnivals as the North Koreans celebrate the thousands of years of their culture	Music continues under voice
5	MS. Low angle. Children with smiling faces, dressed in traditional Chinese-looking costume, dancing in lines and waving at the camera	These children, rehearsing for a street parade in national costume, were certainly enjoying a day off school!	Music still in the background
6	LS. Inside a shop selling radios and television sets. Lots of people browsing the shelves, looking at the goods for sale	While you are in the country you will probably want to stock up on electrical goods which are less than half the UK prices.	Music still in the background
7	MS. Low angle. People on an escalator travelling downwards	And for getting around the city there is no better way than letting the train…	Same music still in the background
8	Same music still in the background	…take the strain. With its clean and efficient service, the P'yongyang tubes certainly have a thing or two…	Same music still in the background
9	LS. Low angle. Still in the underground, people pass in front of a huge and colourful painting on the wall. It looks like the same man as we saw in the statue	…to teach our own London Underground. Down here you get colourful paintings not graffiti on the walls	Same music still in the background, fades up for a few seconds to end the piece

Mini Assignment 6

On what sort of programme would you expect to see the first of these extracts appearing? What are the clues that lead you to that conclusion? Now decide what sort of programme might contain the second extract and how you can tell this.

From Mini Assignment 6 you can see that the choices made about what goes on the soundtrack are as important as the choice of picture that accompanies them. In our example, even something which people wouldn't necessarily notice as they watch it – the sound effects and music – can subtly change the meaning. By choosing to keep the lively pipe and chime bar music going on throughout the piece in the second extract, a very different mood is set up than the sombre military music of the first piece. In each case, the music reinforces what the voice is saying.

So who chooses what goes on the soundtrack? Well the director will certainly give clear instructions as to what should be laid down, in close collaboration with the editor. The editor will then prepare a **dubbing chart** which will go to the **dubbing mixer** who is responsible for implementing the decisions.

Sound sources

There are a limited number of sound sources for the dubbing mixer to work with:

Synchronised sound is recorded at the same time as the picture and goes to the dubbing mixer together with the pictures. This is mainly the dialogue spoken by characters in a soap opera, for example, or the commentary of a news reporter. In our North Korea extract there is nothing which is obviously synchronised sound. Even the sound of the train wheels in shots 1 and 2 in each extract, or the chatter in the electrical goods shop in shot 6 of the first extract could have been dubbed on afterwards.

Voice-over sound needs to be dubbed on to the picture sequences. In the North Korea pieces, both the voices have been added afterwards. The dubbing chart will make sure that the voice-over places words against appropriate pictures. There wouldn't be much point talking about the wonderful skiing opportunities offered in Glencoe if what we saw on the screen was the green, heather-clad mountains of Glencoe in summer. Sometimes the exact moment at which a word emphasises a cut will have been carefully planned. In shot 2 of the first North Korea piece, the placing of the words "Kim Il Sung" just at the point that we see the statue tells us that the statue is not any old North Korean but the ruthless dictator himself.

Sound effects will also usually be added at the dubbing stage. If you want the sound of one person's fist hitting the jaw of another you will add it on afterwards – for two reasons. First, fight sequences are carefully planned so that no one actually gets physically hurt, so there would be no sound. Second, even if the fist did hit the jaw, the sound would only be a dull thud. Adding a juicy smack as the punch goes in will make it much more dramatic.

Sound effects can be further sub-divided into two types. There are those which directly match actions or events on the screen. The example of the fist hitting the jaw is that type of effect. There are also those sounds which are about the scene but don't match anything we are actually seeing. An example might be the sound of sheep baa-ing and birds twittering to accompany a scene set in the countryside, or traffic noise and car horns dubbed on to a scene in someone's city centre flat. These sorts of sound effect are called ambient sounds. They appear on the soundtrack to back up the illusion that what we are seeing is real rather than something set up to be filmed.

Music is the final source of sound that can be added to the film. In high budget film or television productions, specially composed music will be commissioned for the soundtrack. Alternatively the rights to use well-known pop songs or other music can be bought. The choice of music will be very important. Music is used to make us feel certain emotions as we watch the action on screen. A classic example is the piece of music always used in the *Jaws* films as the build up to a shark attack. Its threatening, urgent feel was very effective in getting the audience on the edge of their seats in anticipation of the shark attack and eventual bloodshed.

Mini Assignment 7

1 Using a film made for the cinema that you have recorded on to video (but preferably not watched for some time), fast forward the tape to a point somewhere in the middle.

2 Make a note of the time display on the video at the point you are starting from. Cover the television screen in some way and play 90 seconds of the film, listing everything you can hear on the soundtrack. (If you find that there is just dialogue at this point, fast forward until you find a part where there are some other sound effects and possibly music as well as dialogue.)

3 Rewind the tape to the your starting point and play the 90 seconds again, adding to your list anything you missed on your first listening.

4 Using the following chart, allocate each item on your list to one of the columns:

Dialogue: How many voices? Can you tell anything about the characters from the sound of their voices?	
Sound effects: where you expect to see something actually matching the sound on the screen	

Mini Assignment 7 *continued*

Ambient sounds which are just there to support the illusion of reality	
Music: What sort of mood or feeling does the music make you feel?	

5 Draw up a storyboard of the shots you imagine will be accompanying the soundtrack. Although what you had in your mind may not match what you actually see when you watch the clip, the sounds alone have created a great deal of meaning for you.

6 Now watch the clip and see how close you were to guessing what the shots looked like.

Screen: summary, assignment and glossary

This summary will help you to identify things you can say in your coursework assignment about film or television material. It is a very brief summary of the main ideas you have studied in this section, so if you are unsure what any of the questions mean you should go back to the appropriate section and re-read it. You certainly shouldn't feel that you have to say something about each point on the list. As a general guide you should start by thinking about any of the techniques which seem to draw attention to themselves. For example, if there are a lot of very quick cuts in a sequence, you might like to suggest what effect this had on you, and why the director and editor might have decided to make you notice the cuts in this way.

Shot types and framing	Why have certain types of shot been chosen? Is there anything unusual about the composition of shots within the frame?
Camera angles and camera and lens movements	Why has the camera been placed or moved in this way?
Editing	Are there any transitions that draw attention to themselves? Why do you think they have been used? How long is each shot held on screen? How would you describe the pace of the sequence? Why do you think it has been paced in this way?
Lighting	Is there anything unusual or "expressive" about the lighting?
Dialogue	What do we learn about the characters from the way they speak? What do we learn about any storyline from what they say to each other, or even directly to us, the audience?
Voice-over	Why has the director decided to have someone else's voice talking directly to us, the audience? What are we being led to think about the pictures by this voice?
Sound effects	What did you hear and why do you think they were put on to the soundtrack?
Music	Why was this particular piece of music chosen? What mood or tone do you think it is setting up?
Visual effects	Have any decisions been made to alter the colour or add in unusual effects that make the pictures "unreal" in any way? What is the likely effect on people who watch it?

Location	Why do you think this location was chosen?
Costume	How do the clothes in the shots add to our understanding of the character?

Use the summary above to help you make notes as you are watching. You should view each piece of material many times before starting to plan your written assignment.

Assignments

Writing your GCSE assignment for the AQA/NEAB syllabus

If you have read through this section carefully and tried out some of the research tasks and mini assignments you will be very well placed to produce a really good course-work assignment based on film or television.

You must remember that this assignment counts for two sets of marks. First, it is given a mark for writing. The particular type of writing must be an analysis, a commentary or a review. There will be particular features of this type of writing that the person marking it will look for.

- They will want to see that you can clearly explain your views about the material you have studied.

- They will want you to do this in a logical and clear way, giving detailed examples to back up your analysis.

You should talk to your teacher after you have planned some initial ideas and check that what you are planning fits the type of writing required.

The second mark you get will be for your "reading" of a piece of film or television. This is where the work you have been doing so far will really help you to analyse the material. The dictionary tells us that "analysis" is breaking something down into parts and examining it minutely to find out how it works. The various features you have looked at in this section, like shot types or angles, lighting effects or music, will be the "parts" of the film or programme which you "break down" and "examine minutely".

The syllabus sets out clearly the sort of thing your essay must include. For example, if your assignment is to be awarded a grade C, you will need to have written about the "style, structure and presentation" of the film or TV material. That will not be a problem because *all of the things you have looked at in this section are to do with those three qualities.*

Another feature of a grade C assignment which the syllabus lists is the need for you to discuss the "effects of language, presentational devices and visual images upon response and opinion". This means that you must discuss how the sound and pictures affect what you think about the material. You might think that this sounds suspiciously like the sort of comments you will already be making about "style, structure and presentation". And you would be right! The very slight difference is that this point takes account of the fact that all media products are made to be seen by an audience.

When you write your assignment there are two main ways in which you can make sure you cover the second part of the grade C criteria concerned with audiences.

- First, you can talk about the way the material affects you. You are a typical audience and whatever you say about the material is completely valid. If that's what it made you think, no one can say you are wrong – as long as you have explained why it makes you think or feel that way.

- Second, you can talk about the way a wider audience might watch the material. Let's take an example. Your assignment might be comparing two television advertisements. Once you have analysed the way in which the advertisements have been put together, you could then move on and say which sorts of people you think the producers had in mind and how you think they hoped to influence "response and opinion".

The coursework assignments

Any of the following suggestions would make good media assignments for your GCSE English coursework. You will notice that they ask you to use very short pieces of film or television. This is to enable you to comment in detail on the way the pieces are put together. Some candidates do enter media assignments which attempt to compare two, or even three, full-length films. It is quite difficult to do this effectively. Very often students attempting these essays spend too long simply telling the story or describing the characters and *not* dealing with all those things we have been looking at in this section.

As a general rule it is a good idea to take very short pieces of film or television and really go into the detail of how they have been put together. What choices have the various people made during the production process and how does this affect what we think about the piece? That question should be at the very front of your mind all the time you are writing.

Another good idea is to compare two short pieces of film or TV. Choosing material with particular differences can help you say more than if you just try to pick apart one advertisement or pop video, for example.

Assignment 1

Comparison of two television advertisements

Choose two television advertisements which are advertising similar but different products. (For example, you could choose two car advertisements or two food products.)

- What differences do you notice in the way that each one has been filmed and edited?

- What do you think each advertisement is trying to make the audience think or feel about its product? How have the director and editor used a variety of film techniques to get this across?

- Who do you think the target audience for these advertisements is and why do you think this is the case?

Assignment 2

Comparison of two pop videos

Choose two pop videos that you think are very different from each other.

- What mood or tone do you think is intended to be set up by each one? Does this change at all at any point in the video?

- How has this mood or tone been achieved by the way the videos have been filmed and edited?

- In what ways do you think the visual material relates to the lyrics of the song?

Who do you think each video was designed to appeal to and why do you think this is the case?

Assignment 3

Comparison of two film trailers
- Choose two film **trailers** that you think are designed to appeal to very different audiences.
- What differences do you notice in the shots used in each trailer and in the way each has been edited?
- Are there any differences in the way the voice-over works in each one?
- What are the key things about the films that you think each trailer is trying to get across to the audience and how do you know this?
- What type of audience do you think the trailer was designed to "hook" and what makes you think this?

(A good source of film trailers is the opening part of commercially hired videos.)

Glossary

backlight	light placed behind the person being filmed. The purpose of this light is to separate the person from the background and give a three-dimensional look to the shot
camera operator	the person who is responsible for recording the action with the camera
close-up (CU)	the CU is where the head and a bit of the shoulders fill the screen. We can tell a great deal about the feelings of the person when a CU is used
credits	list on screen at the end of a film or programme of all the people involved in making it
cut	the cut is where one shot is instantly followed on the screen by another
desaturation (of colour)	a shot or sequence which has a bleached-out effect
director	person with overall responsibility for all details relating to acting, camera work and editing. This person literally "directs the attention of the audience" by the way she or he sets up each shot and builds up the sequences
dissolve	this is where the first shot gradually dissolves and is replaced by the second shot. There will be a moment when both shots are on the screen, before the first one gradually fades away

dolly	a platform for the camera, mounted on wheels so it can run alongside the action
dubbing	the process of adding sound on to the pictures for a film or TV programme
dubbing editor (or **dubbing mixer**)	the person responsible for implementing the dubbing instructions of the director which are written out on a **dubbing chart**
establishing shot	the first shot in a sequence which establishes where it is taking place
expressive lighting	when a shot or sequence has unusual lighting specially designed to give a certain mood or tone
extreme close-up (ECU)	in an ECU, one part of the person completely fills the screen. When an ECU is used it will have a dramatic effect on the person watching
extreme long shot (ELS)	the main thing we see in an ELS will be the setting or location. Any person in an ELS will be very tiny indeed
fade	this can either be a fade in, which is where a blank screen is gradually filled by the incoming shot, or a fade out where the shot gradually fades away leaving a blank screen
fill light	a light placed on the opposite side to the key light and which is less powerful. It literally "fills in" the shadows created by the key light
frame	in film, a frame is actually one individual picture on the strip of film. However it is also a word used to describe the "frame" put on the action by the camera. Just as the frame around a painting provides the edges, so all those things in a film which are "in frame" are what we actually see. If they are not visible they are out of the frame
gallery	in a television studio, the gallery is the control room where the director, vision mixer and other technicians sit watching the monitors which show what every camera has in frame
jump cut	the effect of a jump cut is to make the character on the screen literally "jump" from one place to another. It also makes the person watching jump because it disrupts our illusion that what we are seeing is real life
key light	the main source of light in the shot. It is usually set slightly to one side of the camera and directed at the person being lit
lighting camera person	the chief camera person working on a film who works out the type of lighting which will give the scene the look and feel that the director requires

location	the place where the action happens. If a film is shot "on location" this means it is not in a studio but at an actual place
long shot (LS)	the LS will show the whole of any person who is in the shot and there will be a lot of information about the location where the action is taking place
mid shot (MS)	the MS will show the person with their waist cut off by the bottom of the frame. We will still be able to see some of the background but the person will fill much more of the frame than they do in the LS
monitor	television screens used to show what the cameras are filming
pace	how quickly or slowly the sequence seems to move. This is always controlled at the editing stage and is mainly about the length of time individual shots are kept on screen. Rapid cutting between shots would give a fast pace. It is used in chase sequences, for example, where directors and editors want to excite their audience
pan	moving the camera from left to right or from right to left
point of view (POV) shot	a shot where the camera seems to be the eyes of a character
producer	the overall organiser for a film or television programme. The producer is especially involved in putting the money together which enables things to be made
screenplays	the script for a film or television. They look like play scripts but have more detail about what will appear on the screen as well as all the words that are spoken
sequence	a series of individual shots, when joined together by the editor, form a sequence
shot	one uninterrupted run of the camera or, in the finished and edited film, a piece of action uninterrupted by any sort of edit transition
shot/reverse shot	used when filming conversation between two characters. We see the first character in the shot, then we see the person who they are talking to in the reverse shot
sound effects *+ sound track*	usually added to the soundtrack at the dubbing stage. These can be further sub-divided into two types. There are those which directly match actions or events on the screen. There are also those sounds which are about the scene we are seeing but don't match anything we are actually seeing. These second sorts of sound effect are called **ambient sounds**. They appear on the soundtrack to give greater depth to the illusion that what we are seeing is real rather than something set up to be filmed

special effects	careful planned sequences where dangerous actions (leaping from cliffs, crashing cars, etc.) are carried out. Where a star's character would be undertaking the action, a body double or stunt person stands in for them. The **special effects co-ordinator** is the person who sets up the stunts
steadicam	a special mounting for the camera which is worn by the operator like a jacket. It enables the operator to follow the action without the shot appearing to wobble or shake
storyboard	a set of drawings which show what each shot will look like and how it links to the next one
synchronised sound	any sound which exactly matches actions we are seeing in the pictures. Dialogue spoken by characters will be the main type of synchronised sound. Matching up the words people say to the movement of their lips is called **lip-synching**
tilt	moving the camera upwards or downwards. A tilt is a vertical version of the pan
tracking	moving the camera forwards, backwards or sideways on wheels
trailer	short piece used to promote a film or TV programme
vision mixer	the person responsible for mixing or cutting between cameras in a television studio production
visual effects	effects such as floating figures, spinning images, very bold colours, two or more images superimposed on top of each other, written messages crawling along the top or bottom of the screen which are created in laboratories in the case of film or through video effects equipment for television
voice-over	the use of a voice to explain or expand on what the viewers are seeing on the screen but where we do not see the person who is doing the talking
wipe	the effect of a wipe is to see the first shot chased off the screen by the next shot. Wipes can use all sorts of different patterns to get one shot off and the next on
zoom	using the zoom facility on the lens, the operator can zoom in to appear to be closer to the subject or zoom out to make the subject look further away

Acknowledgements

The author and publishers wish to thank the following for permission to use copyright material:

Abbott Mead Vickers/Guinness p.6, Abbott Mead Vickers/Sainsbury's plc p.61; Automobile Association p.59; BBC p.5, p.80; Bild p.29; BNPDDB Needham/Volkswagen p.79; British Telecommunications plc p.58; Carlton Films p.82; Carlton Television p.81; Crown Copyright p.74; E T Archive p.46, p.56; France Soir p.30; IBM/Chelsea Village plc p.55, p.56; Keycamp Holidays p.51; Kobal Collection/Eon Productions p.87, p.88, p.89, p.107; Land Rover p.9, p.79, p.84, p.89; Martin Phillips Collection p.45; Midland Mainline plc p.44; Mirror Syndication International p.12, p.15, p.17, p.18, p.19, p.31, p.33, p.36, p.42; Moviestore Collection p.79, p.92; News International p.13, p.37, p.70; Nike p.59; North News and Pictures p.25, p.26; Oxford Design and Illustration (artwork developed from *Grammar of the Shot* by Roy Thompson, Focal Press, 1998, p.99) p.91; Oxford Design and Illustration (artwork developed from Robert Watson, *Film and Television in Education*, courtesy of Falmer Press) p.96; Oxford Design and Illustration (artwork developed from *The Camera Assistant* by Douglas C. Hart, Focal Press, 1996, p.300) p.92; Oxford Design and Illustration p.100, p.108 p.110; Oxford Mail p.28; Pearson Television p.80, p.97; Pinewood Studios/Eon Productions p.85, p.86; Save the Children p.49; Sylvia Corday Photo Library p.48; The Conde Nast Publications Ltd p.69; Tom Phillips Photography p.50, p.53, p.90, p.95. p.105, p.106; Topham Picturepoint p.23; United News and Media p.38; Volvo p.54.

The author and publishers are also grateful to the following for permission to reproduce text materials:

Carlton Television for an extract (page 83) from Arther Hopcraft's screenplay of Rebecca by Daphne du Maurier (Chameleon, 1997); Mirror Syndication International for an extract (page 18) from an article in *The Mirror* (25 November 1998); Pearson Television for the reproduction of the script extract (pp. 98–99) from *Neighbours*; Phaidon Press for an extract (page 47) from *Art Directing Photography* by Hugh Marshall (1989).